The World Waits For Your Leadership!

Advanced Strategies to Lead in a Competitive World

The World Waits for Your Leadership!

Leadership skills

Jose Rodríguez Vega.
Human Resources Specialist,
Project Management Engineering,
other books,
Your time,
The Leader's Prompt

April 2024
© Biosfera360+

Table of Contents

Introduction. 6

Chapter 1: Fundamentals of leadership. 9

Definition of leadership. 10

Importance of leadership in organizations. 12

Key qualities of a leader. 14

Differences between leadership and management. 16

Chapter 2: Leadership styles. 19

Autocratic leadership. 20

Democratic leadership. 22

Transformational leadership. 25

Situational leadership. 27

Contemporary approaches in leadership. 30

Chapter 3: Effective communication. 35

Importance of communication in leadership. 36

Verbal communication skills. 38

Non-verbal communication skills. 41

Communication in difficult situations. 44

Chapter 4: Team management. 47

Formation of effective teams. 48

Delegation of tasks and team empowerment. 51

Motivation of team members. 54

Conflict resolution within the team. 58

Chapter 5: Decision Making 63

Decision-making process. 64

Decision making under pressure. 67

Ethical decision making. 69

Chapter 6: Ethical leadership. 73

Importance of ethics in leadership. 74

Ethical principles for leaders: integrity, responsibility and transparency. 76

How to handle ethical dilemmas in business leadership. 79

Chapter 7: Personal and professional development. 83

Importance of continuous leader development. 84

Permanent learning. 87

Development of leadership skills. 90

Balance between work and personal life. 93

Chapter 8: Personal Development and Self-knowledge. 97

Emotional self-awareness. 98

Time management and prioritization. 100

Resilience and stress management. 103

Creativity and lateral thinking. 105

Emotional intelligence development. 108

Chapter 9: Building and Managing Relationships. 111

Development of professional networks. 112

Negotiation and conflict resolution. 115

Empathy and interpersonal understanding........................... 118

Coaching and mentoring. 120

Building high-performance teams. 123

Chapter 10: Innovation and Organizational Change 127

Innovation culture. 128

Change management.. 131

Strategic thinking.. 133

Adaptability and flexibility.. 136

Promotion of experimentation and learning........................ 139

Conclusion. 142

Introduction.

In the field of business leadership, the search for excellence is a constant. Leaders from all spheres are in a continuous search for knowledge, skills and perspectives that help them meet the challenges of a constantly evolving business world. This book aims to be your guide on this journey, offering an in-depth and applied exploration of a wide range of topics related to leadership and management.

From the fundamental definition of leadership to strategies for managing organizational change, each chapter of this book dives into a key aspect of business leadership, offering valuable insights and practical tools that you can apply in your own journey as a leader. Whether you're leading a small team at an emerging startup or leading a large international corporation, you'll find the concepts and advice presented here relevant and applicable.

The book begins with an exploration of the very meaning of leadership. What makes an effective leader? How is leadership different from simply managing people? These fundamental questions set the stage for the rest of the book, providing a solid foundation on which to build an effective leadership approach.

As we progress, we dive into the importance of specific leadership skills, from effective communication to conflict resolution and ethical decision making. Each chapter examines a particular topic in detail, providing practical examples and useful exercises to help you develop and strengthen those skills in your own business context.

But leadership is not just about individual skills; It's also about building and leading effective teams. Throughout this book, we will explore how to build cohesive, high-performing teams, how to foster collaboration and innovation, and how to lead successfully in times of change and adversity.

Additionally, we recognize the importance of self-reflection and personal growth in the leader's journey. From developing emotional intelligence to work-life balance, we explore how leaders can cultivate their own well-being and effectiveness as they lead others to success.

Throughout each chapter, you'll find inspiring examples of real leaders who have faced challenges similar to yours and found innovative ways to overcome them. From transformational leaders in history to contemporary executives leading companies that are leaders in their industry, these stories offer valuable insight into what is possible when effective leadership is applied.

This book is not intended to be a quick fix or a foolproof recipe for success. Rather, it is a tool you can use to strengthen your leadership skills, broaden your perspective, and find inspiration on the journey toward excellence in business leadership. With each page, we invite you to reflect on your own leadership approach, identify areas for improvement, and commit to an ongoing journey of learning and growth.

Chapter 1:
Fundamentals of leadership.

Definition of leadership.

Leadership, a fundamental piece in the fabric of modern organizations, transcends mere human resource management to become a complex art of influence and direction. Defining leadership involves entering a territory that goes beyond formal roles and assigned responsibilities; It is understanding the ability to inspire, motivate and guide others towards the achievement of common goals.

At its purest essence, leadership is the ability to influence the behavior and actions of others, not only through formal authority, but also through example, vision, and empathy. An effective leader not only dictates orders, but inspires his team to reach their full potential, cultivating an environment of trust, collaboration and mutual growth.

The distinction between leadership and simple management lies in the depth and breadth of impact. While management focuses on coordinating resources and executing tasks, leadership involves creating visions, aligning values, and inspiring people. A manager can ensure that things get done, but a leader goes further, motivating his team to do the right thing and pursue excellence with passion and commitment.

For some, leadership manifests itself in the ability to make difficult decisions in times of uncertainty, showing courage and resilience in the face of adversity. For others, it lies in the ability to communicate a compelling vision that inspires others to move forward even in times of change and challenge. However, regardless of differences in style and approach, all leaders share a fundamental quality: the ability to positively influence those in their charge and generate a significant impact on their environment.

Leadership transcends the limits of organizational structures and manifests itself in all areas of life. From the team leader in a company to the mentor in a community, leadership is defined by the ability to inspire, guide and empower others to reach their full potential and achieve the common good. In this sense, leadership is not just a set of skills and techniques, but a deep commitment to personal growth and service to others.

Importance of leadership in organizations.

The importance of leadership in organizations is undeniable and transcends the limits of any industry or sector. Effective leadership is not only a key factor in a company's success, but it can also make the difference between sustainable growth and stagnation.

To fully understand the importance of leadership in organizations, it is useful to analyze examples of successful companies that have been shaped by visionary and competent leaders. An emblematic case is that of Apple Inc., under the leadership of Steve Jobs. Jobs was not only an innovator in the technology space, but he also exemplified a unique and visionary leadership style that transformed the technology industry. His ability to inspire his team, foster creativity, and maintain high standards of excellence contributed greatly to Apple's success as one of the most innovative and successful companies in the world.

Another notable example is Starbucks Corporation, led by Howard Schultz. Schultz not only built a globally recognized brand, but also distinguished himself with his people-centered approach and commitment to corporate social responsibility. His values-focused leadership, which prioritized both employees and customers, was instrumental in establishing a strong organizational culture and a shared sense of purpose among everyone in the company.

These examples illustrate how effective leadership can positively impact the success and longevity of an organization. Beyond simply directing and supervising, an effective leader has the ability to inspire employees, align them with the company's vision and values, and unlock their full potential. This not only leads to greater engagement and job satisfaction, but also drives innovation, productivity, and long-term growth.

Additionally, effective leadership is critical to navigating the challenges and turbulence that inevitably arise in the business environment. In times of rapid change and disruption, a strong leader can provide direction, stability and confidence to his team, helping them adapt and thrive in new conditions.

The importance of leadership in organizations is fundamental for business success. Effective leaders are catalysts of change, drivers of innovation, and builders of strong organizational cultures. By analyzing examples of successful companies, it is clear that competent and visionary leadership is an invaluable asset that can make the difference between success and failure in the business world.

Key qualities of a leader.

The key qualities of a leader are the heart and soul of your ability to influence, inspire and guide others to success. By reflecting on the qualities you admire in the leaders you have known or studied, you embark on a journey of self-exploration that will allow you to identify areas of personal development and growth on your own path to leadership.

One of the most admired qualities in a leader is integrity. Leaders of integrity are honest, ethical, and consistent in their actions and decisions. Their transparent and trustworthy behavior creates an environment of trust and mutual respect between themselves and their followers. Reflect on how you can cultivate integrity in your own leadership, committing to act honestly and ethically in all your interactions and decisions.

Another essential quality is the ability to communicate effectively. Effective leaders are skilled communicators who can convey their ideas clearly, concisely, and persuasively. They know how to actively listen to their employees and foster an environment of open and respectful dialogue. Consider how you can improve your verbal and non-verbal communication skills, as well as your ability to listen to and understand your team's needs and concerns.

The ability to inspire and motivate others is also a fundamental quality of an effective leader. Inspiring leaders have a clear vision of the future and can communicate that vision compellingly, stimulating passion and commitment in their team. Reflect on your own goals and aspirations, and how you can articulate an inspiring vision that resonates with your team's shared values and objectives.

Empathy is another essential quality in leadership. Empathic leaders are sensitive to the needs and feelings of others, and can relate and connect emotionally with their team. Practice putting yourself in other people's shoes and understanding their unique perspectives and experiences. Cultivate strong, authentic relationships with your team members, demonstrating empathy and understanding at all times.

The ability to make difficult decisions and take responsibility is also crucial in leadership. Leaders must be willing to face challenges and make difficult decisions even in times of uncertainty and pressure. Reflect on how you can develop your ability to evaluate complex situations, make informed decisions, and take responsibility for outcomes.

The key qualities of a leader are critical to their success and the success of their team and organization. By reflecting on the qualities you admire in other leaders, you can identify areas of strength and areas for improvement in your own leadership. Commit to developing these qualities throughout your career as a leader, and you will see your ability to influence, inspire, and guide others to success strengthen and expand over time.

Differences between leadership and management.

Exploring the differences between leadership and management is essential to understanding how each role uniquely contributes to the functioning and success of an organization. Although both terms are often used interchangeably, they represent two different but complementary aspects of the management process.

At its core, management focuses on the coordination and administration of resources and processes to achieve specific objectives within a given time frame. Managers are responsible for planning, organizing, directing and controlling the daily activities of an organization to ensure efficiency and the achievement of established goals and objectives.

On the other hand, leadership focuses on inspiring, motivating and guiding people towards achieving a shared vision. Leaders are visionaries who articulate strategic direction, foster innovation, and create an environment of trust and collaboration in which team members can reach their full potential.

A fundamental difference between leadership and management lies in the focus on people versus the focus on processes and systems. While management focuses on operational efficiency and meeting organizational objectives, leadership focuses on inspiring and empowering people to give their best and contribute to the success of the organization in a meaningful way.

Another key difference is the time horizon. While management tends to focus on the short term and executing immediate tasks and processes, leadership takes a long-term perspective and focuses on creating and executing a compelling and compelling vision that inspires others to move forward.

Additionally, a manager's responsibilities are typically more prescriptive and defined, with a focus on supervising and coordinating specific activities, while a leader's responsibilities are more fluid and oriented toward developing people and achieving strategic objectives. long term.

Despite these differences, it is important to recognize that leadership and management are two sides of the same coin and can complement each other in an effective organization. While managers provide the structure and stability necessary for the daily functioning of the organization, leaders inspire and motivate people to push boundaries and reach new levels of excellence.

While there are significant differences between leadership and management in terms of focus, responsibilities, and time horizon, both play critical roles in the success of an organization. Recognizing and leveraging each other's strengths can help create a strong, effective management team that can meet challenges and seize opportunities in an ever-changing business environment.

Chapter 2:
Leadership styles.

Autocratic leadership.

Autocratic leadership, characterized by centralized decision making and complete control by the leader, is a leadership style that can be effective in certain specific circumstances. While this approach may seem restrictive and authoritarian, there are situations where autocratic leadership may be the most appropriate option to address urgent challenges or crisis situations where a quick and decisive response is required.

Imagine a technology company facing a serious technical issue that threatens to severely impact the delivery of a crucial project for an important client. In this situation, time is of the essence and the pressure to resolve the problem quickly and effectively is immense. In such circumstances, an autocratic leader may be the most suitable choice to take control and direct the team towards a quick and efficient solution.

The autocratic leader would assume total control of the situation, making decisions without consulting the team and directly directing the actions to follow. He would establish a clear action plan and define specific roles and responsibilities for each team member. Doing so would eliminate any confusion or indecision, allowing the team to fully focus on solving the problem without distractions.

The team dynamic under autocratic leadership in this situation would be highly structured and action-oriented. The team members would follow the leader's instructions in a disciplined manner and execute assigned tasks accurately and efficiently. Communication would be primarily one-way, with the leader providing clear instructions and regular updates on progress toward solving the problem.

While autocratic leadership can be effective in crisis situations or when a quick and decisive response is needed, it can also have its disadvantages. This leadership style can undermine team morale and breed resentment among members who may feel left out of the decision-making process. Furthermore, a lack of participation and collaboration can limit creativity and innovation, which could negatively affect the quality of the proposed solutions.

However, it is important to recognize that autocratic leadership is not suitable for all situations and should not be used indiscriminately. In more stable environments and in situations where team participation and creativity are valued, a more democratic or participatory approach may be more appropriate and effective in fostering a collaborative and empowered work environment.

Autocratic leadership can be an effective option in specific situations where a quick and decisive response is required. In the aforementioned example, autocratic leadership would allow the team to quickly address the technical problem and ensure successful delivery of the project to the client. However, it is important to keep in mind the limitations of this leadership style and use it with caution, recognizing that each situation requires a unique leadership approach tailored to specific circumstances.

Democratic leadership.

Let's imagine a scenario where I am leading a team and decide to implement a democratic leadership approach to decision making. This approach is characterized by encouraging the active participation of all team members in the decision-making process, allowing their opinions and contributions to be heard and taken into account before reaching a final conclusion.

To successfully implement a democratic leadership approach, the first thing I would do is establish an inclusive and trusting work environment where all team members feel comfortable expressing their ideas and opinions without fear of retaliation or judgment. This would require establishing open and transparent communication from the beginning, where mutual respect is encouraged and diversity of perspectives is valued.

Once this work environment is established, I would involve team members in the decision-making process from the beginning. Rather than unilaterally imposing my own ideas or decisions, I would encourage all team members to contribute their knowledge, experiences, and views on the topic at hand. This could be achieved through regular team meetings, brainstorming sessions and open discussions where idea sharing and collaboration are encouraged.

Additionally, it would provide team members with the information and resources necessary to make informed and informed decisions. This could involve sharing relevant data, previous research, or any other relevant information that can help the team fully understand the scope and implications of the decisions being considered.

As the decision-making process unfolds, I would act as a facilitator and mediator, ensuring that all voices are heard and that a team consensus is reached. This might involve moderating discussions, resolving conflicts, and helping the team reach compromises when differences of opinion arise.

Once a team consensus has been reached, I would ensure that all decisions are communicated clearly and transparently to all team members.

This would help ensure that everyone is aligned and committed to the decisions made, which would promote greater team cohesion and collaboration.

To further encourage participation from all team members, I would establish a continuous feedback and review system where team members are encouraged to share their opinions and suggestions on how to improve the decision-making process in the future. This could involve conducting team satisfaction surveys, regular feedback meetings, or any other mechanism that allows team members to express their thoughts and feelings constructively.

Implementing a democratic leadership approach to decision-making in a team requires establishing an inclusive and trusting work environment, encouraging the active participation of all team members, and facilitating a transparent and collaborative decision-making process. By doing so, the collective knowledge and experience of the team can be leveraged to make more informed and effective decisions, which will promote greater cohesion and success in the overall team.

Transformational leadership.

Transformational leadership is a leadership style that goes beyond simply managing and leading teams. It focuses on inspiring and motivating followers to achieve higher goals and create positive change in their environment. Throughout history, there have been numerous examples of transformational leaders whose impact endures over time, inspiring entire generations and leaving a lasting legacy of change and progress.

One of the most prominent examples of transformational leadership is that of Mahatma Gandhi. Gandhi was an Indian leader who led the country to independence from British rule through nonviolent resistance and civil disobedience. His focus on peaceful resistance and his dedication to the cause of social justice inspired millions of people in India and around the world to join his fight for freedom and equality. Gandhi managed to motivate his followers towards a common goal through their emotional connection with his values and principles, and his ability to mobilize the masses in a peaceful and determined manner.

Another notable example of transformational leadership is that of Nelson Mandela. Mandela was a South African leader who fought against the apartheid regime and advocated for racial equality and reconciliation in his country. Despite spending 27 years in prison, Mandela never lost faith in his vision of a free and democratic South Africa. His resilience and determination inspired people of all races and social classes to unite in the fight against injustice and oppression. Mandela managed to unite his divided nation towards a common goal of peace and reconciliation, setting a lasting example of transformational leadership in history.

In business, Steve Jobs is widely recognized as a transformational leader who revolutionized the technology industry with his innovative vision and passionate approach. As co-founder of Apple Inc., Jobs led the company to success with iconic products such as the iPhone and iPad. His visionary leadership style and his ability to inspire his team toward excellence contributed greatly to Apple's success as one of the most innovative companies in the world. Jobs managed to motivate his followers towards a common goal of creating revolutionary products that changed the way we live and work, leaving a lasting legacy in the world of technology and business.

In each of these examples, transformational leaders demonstrated the ability to inspire and motivate their followers toward a common goal by articulating a compelling vision and adopting a passionate and determined approach. His leadership transcended borders and barriers, uniting people of different backgrounds and perspectives in the pursuit of positive and meaningful change in their communities and the world at large.

Transformational leadership is based on leaders' ability to create meaningful change in their followers, inspiring them to push boundaries and reach their full potential. By focusing on a shared vision and mobilizing people toward a common goal, transformational leaders can create lasting impact that transcends the limitations of time and space. Ultimately, transformational leadership is a powerful catalyst for positive change and progress in all areas of life, leaving a lasting legacy of inspiration and motivation for future generations.

Situational leadership.

Situational leadership is a dynamic approach that recognizes that there is no single leadership style that is effective in all situations. Instead, it involves adapting leadership style to the specific needs and individual abilities of team members, as well as the changing demands of the environment and circumstances.

To illustrate how I would adapt my leadership style based on the individual needs and abilities of my team members in different situations,

I will consider several hypothetical scenarios and how I would approach each of them:

Situation 1: New team member with little experience: If a new member joins the team with little experience in the field or organization, she would adopt a more directive leadership style at first. I would provide clear orientation, detailed instructions, and close supervision to help the new member become familiar with her responsibilities and her work environment. As she gains more experience and confidence, she would gradually transition to a more delegative style, giving her more autonomy and responsibility.

Situation 2: Complex and urgent project: In a complex and urgent project where rapid decision making and action is required, I would take a more authoritarian or directive approach. You would assign clear roles and responsibilities, set clear deadlines and expectations, and make decisions quickly and decisively to keep the project on track. However, I would remain receptive to the team's ideas and input to ensure effectiveness and efficiency in project execution.

Situation 3: Conflict between team members: If a conflict arose between team members, I would adopt a more facilitative and problem-solving leadership style. I would listen to the concerns of both parties impartially, facilitate an open and constructive discussion to identify the underlying causes of the conflict, and we would work together to find a mutually beneficial solution. Furthermore, it would reinforce the importance of collaboration and teamwork to overcome challenges and achieve our common goals.

Situation 4: Highly motivated and competent team member: If I have a highly motivated and competent team member, I would adopt a more delegative or supportive leadership style. I would recognize her abilities and strengths, and give her the freedom and autonomy to make decisions and lead initiatives within the team. I would act as a mentor and support resource, providing guidance and feedback when necessary, but allowing the team member to take the initiative and exercise leadership of it effectively.

In each of these scenarios, my goal would be to adapt my leadership style to meet the individual needs and team skills, as well as the specific demands of the situation. I recognize that there is no one-size-fits-all approach that will be effective in all circumstances, so I am willing to be flexible and adjust my leadership style as necessary to maximize overall team performance and success.

Situational leadership involves adapting leadership style to individual needs and team abilities, as well as the changing demands of the environment and circumstances. By being aware of individual differences and unique situations, I can maximize the team's potential and guide it toward achieving our common goals.

Contemporary approaches in leadership.

Contemporary approaches to leadership reflect the changing dynamics of the business environment and the new expectations of leaders in the 21st century. These approaches focus on developing adaptive and strategic skills to lead teams effectively in an increasingly complex and diverse world. Let's explore some of the main contemporary approaches in leadership and how they are influencing current practice:

Transformational Leadership: This approach focuses on inspiring and motivating followers to reach higher levels of performance and achievement. Transformational leaders articulate an inspiring vision, foster innovation and change, and create a collaborative and empowered work environment. Examples of transformational leaders include Nelson Mandela, who inspired an entire country towards reconciliation and positive change, and Steve Jobs, who transformed the technology industry with his bold vision and innovative approach.

Authentic Leadership: This approach focuses on the leader's authenticity, transparency, and integrity. Authentic leaders are genuine in their actions and communications, and act in accordance with their core values and beliefs. They foster relationships of trust and mutual respect with their followers, which promotes a sense of belonging and commitment in the team. Examples of authentic leaders include Michelle Obama, who has been praised for her authenticity and empathy, and Warren Buffett, whose honesty and openness have been critical to her success in business.

Situational Leadership: This approach recognizes that there is no single leadership style that is effective in all situations. Instead, leaders must adapt their leadership style based on the individual needs and abilities of team members, as well as the changing demands of the environment and circumstances. This approach encourages flexibility and adaptability in leadership, allowing leaders to respond effectively to a variety of situations and challenges. Examples of situational leaders include Jeff Bezos, who has demonstrated a unique ability to adapt and evolve in an ever-changing business environment, and Angela Merkel, who has demonstrated situational leadership skills when facing complex crises and challenges in European politics.

Servant Leadership: This approach focuses on putting the needs and well-being of followers first. Servant leaders care about the personal and professional development and growth of their followers, and actively work to support and empower them to reach their full potential. This approach promotes a culture of collaboration, empathy and caring in the workplace, contributing to a positive and productive work environment. Examples of servant leaders include Martin Luther King, whose dedication to service and the well-being of others inspired a national peaceful resistance movement in the United States, and Howard Schultz, whose focus on the well-being of employees and communities has been instrumental. for the success of Starbucks.

Adaptive Leadership: This approach focuses on developing leaders' ability to adapt and respond effectively to challenges and rapid changes in the business environment. Adaptive leaders are agile and flexible in their thinking and action, and can lead successfully in situations of uncertainty and complexity. This approach promotes innovation, resilience and the capacity for continuous learning in leadership. Examples of adaptive leaders include leaders, whose ability to innovate and pivot quickly has been critical to the success of their companies, who demonstrated adaptive and resilient leadership in the face of challenges such as the COVID-19 pandemic.

Contemporary approaches to leadership reflect the evolving expectations of leaders in the 21st century. These approaches focus on developing adaptive and strategic skills to lead teams effectively in an increasingly complex and diverse world. By understanding and applying these approaches, leaders can inspire, motivate, and guide their teams to success in an ever-changing business environment.

Chapter 3:
Effective communication.

Importance of communication in leadership.

The importance of communication in leadership cannot be underestimated; It is the glue that binds a team and the catalyst that drives productivity and engagement. Reflecting on how clear and effective communication can influence the productivity and commitment of my team is essential to developing effective leadership and strengthening relationships within the group.

First, clear and effective communication sets clear expectations and aligns all team members with common objectives and goals. When leaders clearly communicate what is expected of each team member and how their work contributes to the organization's overall goals, it reduces confusion and fosters a sense of shared purpose. Team members understand their role and responsibilities, allowing them to work more effectively and focused toward achieving established goals.

Additionally, clear and effective communication fosters transparency and trust within the team. When leaders share information openly and honestly, it builds a culture of trust and collaboration where team members feel valued and respected. This creates a positive work environment where you can address problems openly and work together to find solutions, rather than hiding problems or concerns for fear of retaliation.

Clear and effective communication also promotes constructive conflict resolution. When disagreements or misunderstandings arise within the team, open and honest communication allows issues to be addressed quickly and effectively before they escalate. Leaders can facilitate open, respectful conversations where all perspectives are heard and mutual compromise is reached. This prevents conflicts from prolonging or becoming more serious problems that can affect team productivity and engagement.

Additionally, clear and effective communication fosters a collaborative and creative work environment. When leaders encourage team members to share ideas and contributions, innovation is promoted and new solutions to business challenges are generated. Leaders can create safe spaces where diversity of thought is valued and collaboration between different perspectives and skills is encouraged. This can lead to more innovative and effective results that benefit the entire organization.

Finally, clear and effective communication is essential to maintain long-term team commitment and motivation. When leaders regularly communicate with team members, provide constructive feedback, and recognize good work, it reinforces employees' sense of worth and belonging. This increases morale and motivation, resulting in higher productivity and lower employee turnover.

Additionally, open and honest communication during difficult times, such as organizational changes or periods of uncertainty, helps maintain team trust and commitment even in challenging times.

Clear and effective communication is a fundamental pillar of effective leadership. When leaders communicate clearly and openly with their team, they set clear expectations, foster trust and collaboration, resolve conflict constructively, promote innovation, and maintain long-term team engagement and motivation. By reflecting on how clear and effective communication can influence team productivity and engagement, leaders can improve their ability to lead effectively and strengthen relationships within the group.

Verbal communication skills.

Verbal communication skills are critical to effective leadership as they affect how we relate, influence and connect with others in the work environment. These skills are divided into three main components: listening, speaking, and asking effective questions.

Listening: The art of active listening is a crucial skill for any leader. Listening goes beyond simply hearing the words of others; It involves understanding, processing, and responding appropriately to what is being said. To be a good listener, it is important to be fully present in the conversation, showing genuine interest in what the other person has to say. This means eliminating distractions, such as phones or emails, and focusing completely on the person speaking. Additionally, it is important to show empathy and understanding when listening, reflecting the speaker's emotions and concerns to demonstrate that her words have been understood. Practicing active listening strengthens relationships, fosters trust, and promotes a culture of openness and collaboration in the team.

Speaking: The ability to express yourself clearly, concisely and effectively is essential for any leader. When speaking, it is important to convey the message clearly and unambiguously, using clear and easy-to-understand language. Additionally, it is crucial to adapt the tone and style of communication to the target audience, ensuring it is clear and appropriate for the situation. For example, in formal situations, such as high-level meetings or public presentations, it is important to use professional language and maintain a confident, confident posture. On the other hand, in more informal or one-on-one conversations, it is useful to be more relaxed and approachable, fostering an atmosphere of trust and camaraderie. Practicing effective verbal communication helps convey messages clearly and persuasively, facilitating team understanding and engagement.

Ask effective questions: Asking open, relevant and clear questions is a key skill for any leader. Effective questions encourage reflection, exploration and dialogue, leading to deeper understanding and the generation of new ideas and solutions. When asking questions, it is important to be clear and specific about what you are asking, avoiding ambiguous or confusing questions that may lead to misunderstandings. Additionally, it is useful to use open questions that encourage reflection and the expression of ideas and opinions, rather than closed questions that only require short and simple answers. For example, instead of asking "Do you agree with this idea?", you can ask "What do you think about this idea and how do you think we could improve it?" Practicing asking effective questions fosters deeper, more meaningful dialogue, leading to better decision-making and problem-solving on the team.

Verbal communication skills are critical to effective leadership. Practicing active listening, speaking clearly, and asking effective questions are key components to building strong relationships, promoting mutual understanding, and facilitating team collaboration and engagement. By developing these skills, leaders can improve their ability to communicate effectively and successfully lead their teams toward achieving common goals.

Non-verbal communication skills.

Nonverbal communication skills are as crucial as verbal skills in the context of leadership. Our body language, facial expressions, gestures and posture can communicate as much, or even more, than our words. Performing exercises to improve these skills can have a significant impact on how we are perceived as leaders by others.

One of the most basic exercises to improve body language is practicing proper posture. Maintaining an upright and open posture conveys confidence and authority. Also, avoid crossing your arms over your chest, as this can be perceived as defensive or closed off. Practicing proper posture during important meetings and conversations can help others perceive the leader as confident and trustworthy.

Another useful exercise is to practice eye contact. Maintaining eye contact with the people you are speaking to conveys interest and attention. However, it is important not to overdo it and maintain natural and comfortable eye contact. Avoid constantly looking down or to the sides, as this can be interpreted as lack of confidence or avoidance. By practicing eye contact, you can improve connection and empathy with others, strengthening leadership relationships.

Facial expression also plays a crucial role in non-verbal communication. Practicing genuine and appropriate facial expressions can help convey emotions and feelings effectively. For example, smiling genuinely during a conversation can make others feel more comfortable and relaxed, while frowning or showing expressions of frustration can send negative signals and create tensions. By practicing positive and appropriate facial expressions, you can improve your ability to influence and motivate others as a leader.

Gestures are also an important part of non-verbal communication. Practicing open, expansive gestures can convey confidence and enthusiasm, while closed or restricted gestures can be perceived as a lack of interest or commitment. For example, gesturing with your hands while speaking can emphasize important points and keep your audience engaged. However, it is important not to overdo it and keep the gestures proportional to the message and the environment. By practicing appropriate and effective gestures, you can improve clarity and persuasiveness in your communication as a leader.

In addition to these practical exercises, it is also important to observe how body language impacts the perception of our leadership by others. This can be done by asking trusted colleagues for feedback or recording presentation sessions or meetings to review later.

Observing our own body language in action gives us invaluable insight into how we are perceived by others and allows us to identify areas for improvement.

For example, we can notice if we are showing signs of nervousness or lack of confidence, such as swaying, avoiding eye contact, or fiddling with our fingers. We can also observe whether our gestures and facial expressions are aligned with our message and tone of voice, or whether they are sending conflicting signals. By identifying these patterns and behaviors, we can take steps to adjust our body language and improve our effectiveness as leaders.

Improving nonverbal communication skills is essential for leadership success. Practicing exercises to improve body language, such as proper posture, eye contact, facial expressions, and gestures, can have a significant impact on how we are perceived by others. Additionally, observing how our body language impacts others' perception of our leadership provides us with valuable feedback and allows us to adjust our behavior to improve our effectiveness as leaders.

Communication in difficult situations.

Communication in difficult situations is a fundamental skill for any leader. In the business environment, it is inevitable that conflicts and situations will arise that require constructive feedback. Developing effective strategies to handle these situations can make the difference between a team that crumbles under pressure and one that grows stronger through adversity.

One of the key strategies for handling difficult situations is the ability to give constructive feedback. This involves clearly and respectfully communicating areas of improvement or concerns in a team member's performance. When giving constructive feedback, it is important to focus on the specific behavior rather than attacking the person's personality or character. For example, instead of saying, "You're disorganized," you could say, "I've noticed that you've had a hard time keeping up with your tasks lately." Additionally, it is important to provide concrete examples and suggest specific solutions or improvements to address the problem. For example, guidance may be offered on how to improve personal organization, such as establishing to-do lists or prioritizing the most important tasks.

Another important strategy for handling difficult situations is the ability to actively listen. This involves paying full attention to what the other person is saying, without interrupting or judging prematurely. By actively listening, you show respect and empathy toward the concerns and perspectives of others, which can help reduce tension and open the door to more open and constructive communication. Additionally, asking open-ended, thoughtful questions can help deepen your understanding of problems and find mutually satisfactory solutions. For example, you might ask, "Can you explain more about what you are experiencing?" or "What solutions would you suggest to address this problem?"

Another effective strategy for handling difficult situations is to remain calm and in emotional control. It is natural to feel frustrated or upset in conflict situations, but reacting with anger or aggression only makes the situation worse and makes it more difficult to resolve the problem. Instead, it is important to maintain composure and respond in a calm and professional manner. This helps maintain a positive and productive work environment, and shows leadership and maturity in the face of challenges.

Additionally, it is helpful to take a collaborative approach to resolving conflicts. Instead of viewing conflict as a battle that must be won, it is more productive to seek mutually beneficial solutions that meet the needs and concerns of all parties involved. This may involve finding compromises or exploring new ideas and approaches to address the problem. By working together to find solutions, relationships are strengthened and a sense of trust and camaraderie is built within the team.

It is important to remember that the goal of handling difficult situations is not simply to solve the immediate problem, but also to build stronger, longer-lasting relationships on the team. By effectively addressing conflict and providing constructive feedback, you demonstrate commitment to the personal and professional growth and development of team members. This creates a positive and supportive work environment where employees feel valued and motivated to contribute to the success of the organization.

Handling difficult situations requires effective communication skills, including giving constructive feedback, active listening, staying calm and in emotional control, and taking a collaborative approach to resolving conflict. By developing and applying these strategies, leaders can strengthen team relationships, promote a positive and productive work environment, and improve overall organizational performance and success.

Chapter 4:
Team management.

Formation of effective teams.

Building effective teams is a fundamental process for any leader seeking to successfully achieve organizational objectives. Imagining how you would build a diverse but cohesive team, taking into account the skills and personalities of each member, involves a strategic and comprehensive approach that considers both the needs of the organization and the interpersonal dynamics within the team.

First of all, it is important to recognize the importance of diversity in the team. Diversity not only refers to demographic differences such as gender, ethnicity or age, but also diversity of skills, experiences and perspectives. By bringing together individuals with diverse backgrounds and points of view, the decision-making process is enriched, creativity is encouraged, and innovation is promoted.

To build a diverse yet cohesive team, it is crucial to identify each member's individual skills and strengths and how they complement each other. This involves conducting a detailed assessment of each individual's technical skills, interpersonal skills, and work styles. For example, some team members may excel at data analysis and problem solving, while others may be excellent communicators and natural leaders.

By understanding the skills and personalities of each member, you can strategically assign roles and responsibilities to maximize the performance of the team as a whole.

Additionally, it is important to consider the interpersonal dynamics within the team when building cohesive teams. This involves considering each individual's work preferences, as well as their ability to collaborate and work as a team. Some people may prefer to work independently and have a more reserved communication style, while others may thrive in collaborative environments and have a more outgoing personality. By balancing individual needs with team goals, you can create an inclusive and collaborative work environment where each member feels valued and motivated to contribute to collective success.

An effective strategy for building cohesive teams is to foster trust and camaraderie among team members. This can be accomplished through team-building activities such as retreats, recreational activities, or collaborative projects outside of the traditional work environment. These activities not only help strengthen relationships between team members, but also foster a sense of belonging and shared commitment to the goals of the team and the organization as a whole.

Additionally, it is important to set clear and transparent expectations for the team from the beginning. This includes clearly defining the team's objectives, the roles and responsibilities of each member, and expected performance standards. By having a common understanding of what is expected of them, team members can work more effectively and collaboratively toward achieving their shared goals.

It is also crucial to foster a culture of open and honest communication within the team. This involves creating an environment where members feel comfortable expressing their ideas, concerns and suggestions in a constructive manner. By promoting a culture of continuous feedback, you encourage constant learning and improvement within the team, contributing to its cohesion and long-term success.

Finally, it is important that the team leader takes an active and supportive role in the formation and development of the team. This involves providing individualized guidance and mentoring, recognizing and celebrating team achievements, and addressing any conflicts or challenges that may arise quickly and effectively. By leading with empathy and understanding, the connection between the leader and team members is strengthened, contributing to overall team cohesion and performance.

Building a diverse yet cohesive team requires a strategic and comprehensive approach that takes into account the skills and personalities of each member, as well as the interpersonal dynamics within the team. By identifying and capitalizing on individual strengths, fostering trust and communication, setting clear expectations, and providing ongoing support, leaders can create highly effective teams that are well-positioned to achieve success in any challenge they face.

Delegation of tasks and team empowerment.

Delegating tasks and empowering the team are two crucial aspects of effective leadership. The ability to strategically assign responsibilities and provide the support necessary for team members to succeed not only frees up time and resources for the leader, but also fosters the professional growth and development of employees, thereby strengthening the team as a whole. set.

To delegate responsibilities effectively, it is important to start by understanding the individual strengths, skills, and abilities of each team member. This involves conducting an honest and detailed assessment of each individual's technical skills, interpersonal skills, and prior experience.

By understanding the strengths and limitations of each member, the leader can assign tasks strategically, ensuring that each task is aligned with the skills and abilities of the assigned person.

Additionally, it is important to set clear and realistic expectations for each delegated task. This includes clearly defining objectives and expected results, delivery times, and any additional resources or support the team member may need to complete the task successfully. By setting clear expectations from the beginning, you reduce the chance of misunderstandings or mistakes and increase the likelihood of success.

Once responsibilities have been assigned, it is crucial to provide the support necessary for team members to be successful. This may include providing appropriate resources and tools, such as training, guidance or access to relevant information and experts. Additionally, it is important to be available to answer questions, provide feedback, and offer additional guidance as needed. By providing a supportive and trusting environment, team members are empowered to take responsibility for their tasks and make informed decisions to achieve established goals.

It is also important to foster a collaborative work environment where team members feel safe to share ideas, solve problems and seek help when necessary.

This may involve encouraging open communication and collaboration among team members, as well as recognizing and celebrating individual and collective achievements. By creating a positive and supportive work environment, you strengthen the team's sense of belonging and commitment, contributing to their overall success.

Additionally, it is important to continue monitoring the progress and performance of team members as they complete their assigned tasks. This may involve scheduling regular follow-up meetings to review progress, address any issues or challenges that arise, and provide additional guidance as needed. By staying informed about the team's progress, the leader can identify areas of opportunity to provide additional support and ensure the team is on track to achieve its goals.

Lastly, it is crucial to recognize and celebrate the team's achievements and successes. This may include publicly recognizing work well done, offering rewards or incentives for exceptional performance, and providing professional growth and development opportunities for those who demonstrate outstanding commitment and performance. By recognizing and rewarding team effort and dedication, team members' sense of worth and motivation is reinforced, contributing to their job satisfaction and long-term retention.

Delegating tasks and empowering the team are fundamental aspects of effective leadership. By strategically assigning responsibilities and providing the support necessary for team members to succeed, you free up time and resources for the leader, encourage employee professional growth and development, and strengthen the team as a whole. By setting clear expectations, providing resources and support, encouraging collaboration and recognition, and monitoring team progress and performance, the leader can create a positive and productive work environment where team members feel valued, motivated, and empowered. to achieve success.

Motivation of team members.

The motivation of team members is essential to achieve success in any company. A motivated and engaged team is not only more productive, but also more willing to face challenges and work together to achieve common goals. Developing an effective plan to recognize and reward team achievements can have a significant impact on their motivation and commitment.

The first step in developing a recognition and rewards plan is to identify the achievements and behaviors you want to encourage in the team. This may include achieving specific goals, overcoming challenges, effective collaboration, innovation, or any other significant contribution to the success of the team and the organization as a whole. By establishing clear and specific criteria for recognition and rewards, you provide clear guidance on what is valued and expected of team members.

Once recognition and reward criteria are established, it is important to select appropriate forms of recognition and reward that are meaningful and motivating for the team. This may include public recognition in team meetings or internal communications, providing tangible rewards such as bonuses or gifts, or developing career growth and development opportunities such as promotions or special training. By adapting the forms of recognition and reward to individual preferences and team needs, their impact and effectiveness on motivation and commitment is increased.

In addition to tangible forms of recognition and reward, it is important to note the importance of verbal recognition and sincere praise. A simple "thank you" or "good job" can have a significant impact on team motivation and morale, recognizing and valuing the effort and dedication of team members. By expressing appreciation and recognition regularly and authentically, the emotional connection between the leader and team members is strengthened, contributing to their long-term motivation and commitment.

In addition to recognizing past achievements, it is important to establish a reward system that motivates team members to continue working hard and improving in the future. This may involve establishing clear goals and objectives, with incentives associated with achieving specific results. By linking rewards to concrete performance and results, you create a sense of responsibility and motivation in the team to reach their full potential.

It is also crucial to celebrate the team's achievements collectively, recognizing and valuing each member's contribution to the joint success. This may involve hosting special celebratory events, publishing news in internal newsletters or on corporate social media, or creating formal recognition programs that highlight the team's individual and collective achievements. By celebrating team achievements in a public and shared way, you reinforce the team's sense of belonging and pride, which strengthens their long-term motivation and commitment.

Finally, it is important to remain flexible and adapt the recognition and rewards plan as necessary to meet the changing needs of the team and the organization. This may involve periodically reviewing recognition and reward criteria, incorporating new forms of recognition and reward, or conducting surveys or meetings to gather feedback and suggestions from the team on how to improve the existing plan. By remaining responsive and responsive to the team's needs and desires, you demonstrate an ongoing commitment to their long-term motivation and commitment.

Developing an effective plan to recognize and reward team achievements can have a significant impact on their motivation and commitment. By establishing clear and specific criteria for recognition and rewards, selecting meaningful and motivating forms of recognition and reward, and celebrating team achievements collectively and regularly, the emotional connection between the leader and team members is strengthened, which which contributes to their long-term motivation and commitment. By remaining flexible and responsive to the changing needs of the team, you ensure that the recognition and rewards plan remains effective and relevant as the team grows and evolves.

Conflict resolution within the team.

Resolving conflict within a team is an essential skill for any leader. The inevitable disagreements and tensions in a work environment can negatively impact team dynamics and productivity if not addressed fairly and constructively.

Creating an effective process for addressing and resolving conflict is critical to maintaining a healthy work environment and fostering positive relationships among team members.

First, it is important to establish a work environment that encourages open communication and the honest expression of opinions. By creating a space where team members feel safe to share their concerns and perspectives, you reduce the likelihood that conflicts will escalate or become chronic. Fostering trust and transparency from the beginning creates a solid foundation for addressing conflicts constructively.

The leader must set clear expectations about how conflicts within the team should be addressed. This may include defining a formal process for resolving disputes and communicating this process to all team members. A well-defined process provides clear guidance on how to address conflicts, which can help prevent misunderstandings and ensure everyone is on the same page when issues arise.

A valuable tool in conflict resolution is the skill of active listening. Each team member should feel that their concerns are heard and understood. The leader must facilitate open communication, allowing each party to express his or her point of view without interruption and showing empathy toward his or her perspective.

Active listening not only helps you better understand the nature of the conflict, but also creates an environment in which team members feel valued and respected.

Additionally, it is crucial to address conflicts in a timely manner. Ignoring or postponing conflict resolution can lead to additional tensions and deterioration of team relationships. The leader should intervene as soon as possible after conflict identification to address the problem before it escalates.

The conflict resolution process should include space for all parties to express their views and concerns. This can be carried out through mediation meetings or individual conversations, depending on the nature of the conflict. It is important to provide an environment where team members feel safe to share their feelings and thoughts without fear of retaliation.

Once the perspectives of all parties have been identified and understood, the next step is to find solutions. This involves a collaborative approach to finding common ground and resolving the conflict in a way that is acceptable to all parties involved. In some cases, this may involve compromises or creative solutions that address the concerns of everyone involved.

The leader plays a crucial role in guiding the conflict resolution process and ensuring that the proper steps are followed. This may include providing additional resources, such as communication skills training or outside advice, if necessary. Additionally, the leader must ensure that agreed-upon solutions are implemented and follow up to evaluate their effectiveness over time.

It is important for the leader to model positive and effective conflict resolution behaviors. This includes staying calm, being objective, and focusing on solutions rather than blaming individuals. The leader can also share personal conflict resolution experiences to illustrate how challenges can be overcome and stronger relationships built as a result.

Conflict resolution can also be an opportunity for growth and learning within the team. By addressing conflict constructively, team members can develop communication, empathy, and collaboration skills that strengthen long-term group cohesion.

Resolving conflict within a team is essential to maintaining a healthy and productive work environment. Creating an effective process for addressing and resolving conflict involves establishing a work environment that encourages open communication, defining clear expectations, actively listening to all parties, addressing conflicts in a timely manner, and seeking collaborative solutions.

The leader plays a key role in guiding this process, modeling effective behaviors and ensuring lasting solutions are implemented. By addressing conflict constructively, the team can strengthen its relationships and develop skills that contribute to successful and sustainable performance over time.

Chapter 5:
Decision Making

Decision-making process.

The decision-making process is a fundamental part of management and leadership in any work environment. From solving everyday problems to making high-level strategic decisions, leaders must be able to apply a systematic and rational approach to ensure effective and consistent results. To illustrate this process, I will apply a real problem in a work environment to the decision-making process, from problem identification to solution implementation.

Imagine you are the manager of a sales team at a technology company. Recently, you have noticed a decrease in sales of a specific product, even though it has historically been one of your company's most successful products. After reviewing sales reports and collecting feedback from customers and the sales team, you identify that the problem lies in a defect in the product that is affecting its performance and functionality.

The first step in the decision-making process is to clearly identify and define the problem. In this case, the problem is the decrease in sales of the specific product due to a defect in the product. It is important to fully understand the nature and extent of the problem before proceeding to seek solutions.

The next step is to gather relevant information and analyze all available options. This may involve investigating the nature of the defect, evaluating its impact on product performance, and considering possible solutions to address the problem. In this case, you can gather the product development team and perform additional testing to better understand the root cause of the defect and explore options to correct it.

Once all options have been identified and evaluated, it is time to make a decision. This involves evaluating the risks and benefits of each option and selecting the one that best aligns with the company's objectives and values. In this case, after reviewing the test findings and considering the potential impact on company reputation and customer satisfaction, you decide to proceed with a software update to correct the defect in the product.

After making the decision, it is important to implement and execute the solution effectively. This may involve coordinating with the product development team to implement the software update, communicating the fix to affected customers, and training the sales team on the changes made. It is essential to ensure that the solution is implemented in a timely and efficient manner to minimize any additional impact on sales and customer satisfaction.

Once the solution has been implemented, it is crucial to monitor and evaluate its results. This involves tracking sales of the product in question, collecting customer feedback on the effectiveness of the solution, and making adjustments as necessary. In this case, you can establish specific performance metrics, such as increase in product sales and reduction in customer complaints, to evaluate the long-term success of the solution.

Additionally, it is important to learn from experience and look for opportunities to improve the decision-making process in the future. This may involve conducting a post-mortem review of the problem and solution, identifying areas of improvement in the process, and developing action plans to address any identified deficiencies. By learning from mistakes and constantly looking for ways to improve, you strengthen your decision-making process and increase your company's ability to effectively solve problems in the future.

The decision-making process is essential for addressing problems and resolving conflicts in any work environment. By applying a systematic and rational approach, from problem identification to solution implementation, leaders can make effective decisions that lead to positive and consistent results. By learning from experience and constantly looking for ways to improve, the company's ability to address challenges and seize opportunities in the future is strengthened.

Decision making under pressure.

Decision making under pressure is a critical skill for any leader in today's work environment, where challenges and demands can arise unexpectedly and require quick, effective responses. In a high-pressure situation at work, staying calm and making effective decisions can make the difference between success and failure. Below I will describe how I would confront and address this situation.

First of all, it is essential to stay calm and maintain emotional composure at all times. In high-pressure situations, it is natural to feel overwhelmed or stressed, but it is important not to allow these emotions to cloud judgment or affect the ability to make clear, effective decisions. To achieve this, it is helpful to practice deep breathing and mindfulness techniques to reduce stress and maintain mental clarity.

Once a state of calm has been achieved, the next step is to evaluate the situation objectively and rationally. This involves collecting and analyzing all relevant information available, identifying key issues or challenges and evaluating possible options and courses of action available. It is important not to rush into making impulsive decisions, but rather to take the time to fully understand the situation and consider all possible options.

Once the situation has been assessed, it is time to make a decision. In high-pressure situations, it may be necessary to make quick and decisive decisions, but this does not mean taking shortcuts or ignoring the proper decision-making process. It is important to carefully weigh the risks and benefits of each option and select the one that best aligns with the organization's goals and values.

It is also crucial to clearly communicate the decision made to all relevant parties and ensure that expectations and next steps are understood. Effective communication is key in high-pressure situations to ensure alignment and commitment of everyone involved and minimize confusion or uncertainty.

After making the decision, it is important to continually monitor and evaluate its impact and effectiveness. This may involve tracking results and adjusting approach as necessary to address any issues or challenges that arise. It is important to be flexible and prepared to adapt as the situation evolves and more information is obtained.

Additionally, it is helpful to seek support and guidance from colleagues, mentors, or team members in high-pressure situations. Working collaboratively with others can provide additional perspectives and help generate new ideas and creative solutions. It is important to remember that you are not alone and that there are resources and support networks available to help during difficult times.

Lastly, it is important to learn from experience and look for opportunities to improve in the future. Reflecting on what happened, identifying lessons learned, and developing action plans to address areas of improvement can help strengthen the ability to face and overcome similar challenges in the future. Decision making under pressure is a skill that can be developed and honed over time and practice.

Making decisions under pressure is a critical skill for any leader in today's work environment. Staying calm, evaluating the situation objectively, making effective decisions, and clearly communicating the decisions made are key steps in addressing and overcoming high-pressure situations at work. By learning from experience and looking for opportunities to improve in the future, the ability to face and overcome similar challenges in the future is strengthened.

Ethical decision making.

Ethical decision making is a fundamental aspect of effective leadership in the workplace. Leaders constantly face ethical dilemmas that require careful consideration of moral values and principles, as well as the long-term implications of their actions.

To explore this topic, let's examine some common ethical dilemmas in the workplace and how you would apply ethical principles to make difficult decisions.

One of the most common ethical dilemmas in the workplace is the conflict between loyalty to the company and responsibility to employees. For example, let's say you discover that a member of your team has been involved in dishonest employment practices that could damage the company's reputation if they become public. Should you inform upper management and risk your employee's career, or should you try to resolve the issue internally to protect your team?

In this case, applying ethical principles such as honesty, integrity and responsibility can help you make an informed decision. While company loyalty is important, so is the responsibility to ensure an ethical and respectful work environment. Therefore, you might decide to address the problem internally, offering the employee the opportunity to correct her behavior and take steps to prevent future ethical violations. However, if the employee's behavior is particularly serious or represents a significant risk to the company, you may consider reporting it to senior management for appropriate disciplinary action.

Another common ethical dilemma in the workplace is the balance between maximizing profits for the company and corporate social responsibility. For example, let's say your company is considering outsourcing production to a country with lower labor standards to reduce costs and increase profit margins. Should you make this decision knowing that it could result in the exploitation of overseas workers and damage the company's reputation?

In this case, applying ethical principles such as justice, equity and respect for human rights can guide you towards a more ethical decision. While it is important to maximize profits for the company, it is also important to do so in an ethical and responsible manner. Therefore, you might consider exploring other options, such as improving working conditions at existing facilities or seeking out suppliers that meet ethical labor standards. If outsourcing is still the best option from a business perspective, you could work to ensure safeguards are in place to protect the rights and well-being of offshore workers.

Additionally, making ethical decisions can also involve considering the long-term consequences of your actions. For example, let's say your company is considering launching a new product that you know could have long-term negative health or environmental effects.

Should you go ahead with the product launch knowing these risks, or should you look for safer and more sustainable alternatives?

In this case, applying ethical principles such as caution, responsibility and sustainability can help you make a more ethical and responsible decision. While it is important to maximize profits for the company, it is also important to do so in a sustainable and ethical way in the long term. Therefore, you could choose to delay product launch and work to address identified health or environmental issues, or you could look for safer, more sustainable alternatives that minimize potential risks to people and the planet.

Ethical decision making in the workplace involves applying ethical principles and moral values to resolve difficult dilemmas fairly and responsibly. By carefully considering the ethical implications of your actions and making decisions that respect the rights and dignity of all parties involved, you can create an ethical and respectful work environment that promotes the long-term success of the company and the well-being of all its employees. stakeholders.

Chapter 6:
Ethical leadership.

Importance of ethics in leadership.

The importance of ethics in leadership is fundamental to building strong and trusting relationships both inside and outside an organization. As a leader, your personal and ethical values serve as a moral compass that guides your actions and decisions in the work environment. Reflecting on how these values influence your decisions and how you can maintain integrity at all times is essential to cultivating an ethical and respectful work environment.

First, it is crucial to recognize that as a leader you are a role model for your team and other members of the organization. Your actions and decisions set a precedent for ethical behavior within the company. Therefore, it is important to live by your values and demonstrate integrity in all your interactions and decisions.

One of the keys to maintaining integrity in leadership is to be transparent and honest in your communications. Transparency builds trust and credibility between you and your team, which fosters a work environment where ethical values are valued and respected. This involves sharing information openly and honestly, admitting mistakes when necessary, and clearly communicating your expectations and ethical standards.

Additionally, it is important to establish clear ethical standards and promote an organizational culture based on values. This involves clearly defining and communicating the company's values and ethical principles, and aligning organizational policies and practices with these values. Doing so creates an environment where ethics are valued and all members of the organization are expected to act with integrity at all times.

Another important aspect of maintaining integrity in leadership is making ethical decisions even when you face external or internal pressure to act contrary to your values. This may involve resisting the temptation to take shortcuts or compromise your principles for the sake of success or personal gain. It is important to remember that integrity is non-negotiable and that your actions as a leader have a lasting impact on the company's culture and reputation.

Additionally, it is essential to foster a culture of responsibility and accountability within the organization. This involves recognizing and rewarding ethical behavior, as well as effectively addressing any violations of established ethical standards. By holding all members of the organization accountable for their actions and decisions, you reinforce the commitment to integrity and promote an ethical and healthy work environment.

It is also important to seek guidance and support when faced with difficult ethical decisions. Consulting trusted colleagues, mentors, or outside advisors can provide additional perspectives and help you make informed and ethical decisions. Don't be afraid to ask for help when you need it and remember that you are not alone in your ethical journey as a leader.

The importance of ethics in leadership lies in the impact that your actions and decisions have on the culture and success of the organization. Reflecting on how your personal and ethical values influence your decisions and how you can maintain integrity at all times is essential to cultivating an ethical and respectful work environment. By being transparent and honest in your communications, setting clear ethical standards, making ethical decisions even under pressure, and fostering a culture of responsibility and accountability, you can lead with integrity and build strong, trusting relationships within the organization.

Ethical principles for leaders: integrity, responsibility and transparency.

Ethical principles are the foundation on which effective and responsible leadership is built. Identifying the ethical principles that guide your leadership and communicating and applying them in your team and organization is essential to cultivating an ethical and respectful work environment.

Below, I will explore some common ethical principles that can guide leadership and how they can be communicated and applied in the work environment.

First, honesty and integrity are essential for any ethical leader. Being honest and transparent in all interactions and decisions, and living by the highest ethical standards, sets a powerful example for the team and builds trust and credibility both inside and outside the organization. Clearly communicating your expectations and ethical standards and demonstrating consistency between your words and actions reinforces your commitment to honesty and integrity at all times.

Another important ethical principle is respect for others. As a leader, it is essential to treat all team members and other stakeholders with respect and dignity, regardless of their position or status. This involves actively listening to the concerns and perspectives of others, valuing diversity of opinions and experiences, and promoting an environment where individual differences are respected and celebrated. Communicating and modeling respect in all interactions and decisions promotes an inclusive and collaborative work environment where everyone feels valued and respected.

Furthermore, justice and equity are fundamental ethical principles for effective leadership. This involves treating all team members fairly and equitably, making unbiased, merit-based decisions and ensuring equal opportunities for all. Communicating and enforcing fair and equitable organizational policies and practices, and effectively addressing any forms of discrimination or bias, strengthens the commitment to justice and equity in the organization and promotes a work environment where everyone can reach their full potential.

Responsibility and accountability are also key ethical principles for effective leadership. As a leader, it is important to take responsibility for your actions and decisions, as well as foster a culture of responsibility and accountability throughout the team and organization. This involves acknowledging and correcting mistakes when necessary, learning from experience, and constantly looking for ways to improve and grow. Communicating and modeling responsibility and accountability promotes a work environment where personal and collective responsibility is valued and excellence and growth are continually pursued.

Empathy and compassion are also important ethical principles for effective leadership. As a leader, it is essential to understand and show concern for the needs and concerns of others, and to demonstrate empathy and compassion in all interactions and decisions. This involves actively listening to team members, showing support and understanding in times of difficulty, and creating an environment where well-being and inclusion are encouraged. Communicating and demonstrating empathy and compassion strengthens interpersonal relationships and promotes a work environment where everyone feels valued and supported.

Identifying the ethical principles that guide your leadership and communicating and applying them in your team and organization is essential to cultivating an ethical and respectful work environment. Honesty and integrity, respect for others, justice and fairness, responsibility and accountability, and empathy and compassion are some of the key ethical principles that can guide effective leadership. Communicating and modeling these principles in all interactions and decisions strengthens commitment to ethics and promotes a work environment where everyone can reach their full potential.

How to handle ethical dilemmas in business leadership.

Managing ethical dilemmas in business leadership is a challenge many leaders face in today's work environment. These dilemmas can arise when there are conflicts between what is ethically correct and what may be beneficial to the company or the leader's personal interests.

Developing a solid framework to address these dilemmas and seeking different perspectives and solutions are key steps in making ethical and responsible decisions.

First of all, it is important to establish an ethical framework that serves as a guide for making decisions in difficult situations. This framework may include core ethical principles, such as honesty, integrity, respect, and fairness, as well as specific considerations related to the leader's industry, organizational culture, and personal values. Having a clear framework in mind makes it easier to make ethical decisions in times of conflict.

The next step is to identify and analyze the ethical dilemma in question. This involves fully understanding all parties involved, the possible consequences of different actions and how they relate to the ethical principles set out in the framework. It is useful to ask: What are the values at stake? What ethical principles are relevant in this situation? What are the possible ramifications of each course of action?

Once the ethical dilemma has been discussed, it is important to consult colleagues, mentors, or other stakeholders to obtain different perspectives and opinions. Exchanging ideas and seeking different points of view can help enrich understanding of the problem and consider alternative solutions that may not have been initially considered. Additionally, consulting others can also provide support and guidance in times of indecision or conflict.

After gaining different perspectives, it is important to evaluate each option in light of the ethical principles established in the framework. This involves weighing the potential benefits and risks of each course of action and considering how they align with the values and integrity of the leader and the organization as a whole. It is important to not only consider the short-term impact of each decision, but also the long-term implications for organizational reputation and culture.

Once all options have been evaluated, it is time to make an ethical and responsible decision. This involves selecting the course of action that best aligns with the ethical principles set out in the framework and takes into account the perspectives and opinions of all parties involved. It is important to be clear and transparent in communicating the decision and explaining the reasons behind it, even if not everyone agrees. Transparency and consistency are essential to maintaining trust and respect within the organization.

After making the decision, it is important to reflect on the process and learn from the experience. This involves evaluating how the ethical dilemma was handled, what could have been done differently, and how lessons learned can be applied in the future.

Reflection and continuous learning are essential for the leader's personal and professional growth and development.

Handling ethical dilemmas in business leadership requires a careful and thoughtful approach. Develop a solid ethical framework, identify and analyze the ethical dilemma, consult colleagues or mentors to obtain different perspectives and solutions, evaluate each option in light of established ethical principles, make an ethical and responsible decision, and reflect on the process and Learning from experience are key steps to addressing ethical dilemmas effectively and responsibly. By following these steps, leaders can make ethical decisions that promote integrity, trust, and respect within the organization.

Chapter 7:
Personal and professional development.

Importance of continuous leader development.

Continuous leader development is critical to staying relevant and effective in an ever-changing business environment. The speed at which technologies, market trends, and employee and customer expectations evolve makes it imperative for leaders to commit to a constant process of learning and growth. Creating a personal development plan that includes short- and long-term goals is an effective strategy for improving leadership skills and promoting professional growth. Below, we will explore the importance of this process and how it can be implemented effectively.

First, continuous leader development is essential to stay up to date with the latest trends and best practices in leadership and management. This may include studying new leadership theories and models, learning new skills and competencies, and exploring different approaches to problem solving and decision making. Staying informed about developments in the field of leadership allows you to adapt and respond effectively to emerging challenges in the work environment.

Additionally, ongoing leader development is crucial to cultivating a dynamic and ever-evolving work environment. By committing to your own growth and development, you inspire other team members to do the same. This creates an organizational culture that values learning and fosters a sense of collaboration and continuous improvement throughout the company. A leader who demonstrates a commitment to his or her own development is more likely to inspire and motivate others to do the same.

Creating a personal development plan is an effective way to structure and prioritize your growth and development efforts. This plan should include specific short- and long-term goals that are aligned with your career aspirations and the needs of your current role. By setting clear, measurable goals, you can track your progress over time and adjust your plan as necessary to meet your changing needs.

When designing your personal development plan, it is important to identify areas for improvement and opportunities for growth. This may include developing specific leadership skills, such as effective communication, decision making, conflict resolution, and change management. It may also involve seeking opportunities to gain new experiences and knowledge, such as participating in training and development programs, attending conferences and seminars, and seeking out mentors and coaches to help you achieve your goals.

Additionally, it is important to set realistic and achievable deadlines to achieve your personal development goals. This allows you to maintain the focus and discipline necessary to achieve tangible results over time. By setting milestones and progress markers, you can celebrate your achievements and stay motivated as you move toward your goals.

An important part of any personal development plan is regular self-assessment to assess your progress and identify further areas for improvement. This may involve conducting regular reviews of your goals and adjusting your plan as necessary to keep it relevant and effective. It can also be helpful to solicit feedback from colleagues, mentors, and supervisors to get different perspectives on your performance and areas of development.

Continuous leader development is essential to staying relevant and effective in an ever-changing business environment. Creating a personal development plan that includes short- and long-term goals is an effective strategy for improving leadership skills and promoting professional growth. By committing to your own growth and development, you inspire other team members to do the same and cultivate an organizational culture that values learning and continuous improvement.

Permanent learning.

Lifelong learning is an essential practice for any leader who aspires to grow and adapt in an ever-changing business world. Researching continuous learning opportunities, such as courses, seminars or books, and developing a plan to incorporate learning into your daily routine is essential to staying current and constantly improving your leadership and management skills.

First, it is important to recognize that learning is not limited to a specific time or place, but is a continuous process that occurs throughout life. As a leader, it is essential to maintain a growth mindset and be open to learning from all the experiences and people around you. This involves being willing to question your assumptions, explore new ideas and perspectives, and be open to receiving constructive feedback.

One way to encourage continuous learning is to actively seek professional development opportunities. This may include participating in training and development courses, attending seminars and conferences, and reading relevant books and articles on leadership and management. By exposing yourself to different ideas and approaches, you can expand your knowledge and improve your skills in specific areas of leadership.

Additionally, it is important to develop a plan to incorporate learning into your daily routine. This may involve allocating specific time in your schedule for learning activities, such as reading books or participating in online courses. You can also set clear, measurable learning goals and track your progress over time. By making learning a priority and establishing a system to maintain it regularly, you can ensure that you are constantly improving and growing as a leader.

An effective way to integrate continuous learning into your daily routine is to adopt a learning mindset at work. This involves seeing each challenge or situation as an opportunity to learn and grow. For example, instead of avoiding mistakes or failures, you can see them as opportunities for learning and reflection that will help you improve in the future. By adopting this mindset, you can turn every experience into an opportunity to develop and improve your leadership skills.

Additionally, it is important to make the most of the learning opportunities that arise in the work environment. This may include participating in challenging projects or special assignments that allow you to gain new skills and experiences. You can also look for opportunities to work with talented colleagues and learn from their experience and expertise. By being open to learning from the people around you and making the most of development opportunities at work, you can accelerate your growth and development as a leader.

Another effective strategy to encourage continuous learning is to establish a professional learning network. This involves connecting with other leaders and professionals in your field and sharing ideas, resources, and best practices. You can join professional networking groups, attend industry events, and participate in online communities related to leadership and management. By collaborating with other leaders and professionals, you can gain new perspectives and knowledge that will help you improve your leadership skills.

Lifelong learning is critical to staying relevant and effective as a leader in an ever-changing business environment. Investigating continuous learning opportunities, such as courses, seminars or books, and developing a plan to incorporate learning into your daily routine are key steps to constantly improve your leadership and management skills. By adopting a growth mindset, integrating learning into your daily routine, taking advantage of on-the-job learning opportunities, and establishing a professional learning network, you can ensure that you are constantly improving and growing as a leader.

Development of leadership skills.

Developing leadership skills is a continuous and dynamic process that requires self-awareness, commitment and a well-defined strategy. In an ever-evolving business world, successful leaders recognize the importance of constantly improving their skills to lead effectively. To do this, it is essential to take advantage of resources such as mentoring, coaching and training programs. In this analysis, we'll explore how to identify specific areas of improvement, develop an action plan, and get the most out of these leadership development tools.

The first step in developing leadership skills is honest self-assessment. It is important to reflect on your strengths and weaknesses as a leader and identify specific areas in which you want to improve. This may include communication skills, decision making, time management, conflict resolution, or any other area you consider important to your success as a leader. By being aware of your areas for improvement, you can set clear and measurable goals for your personal and professional development.

Once you have identified your areas for improvement, the next step is to develop an action plan to acquire new skills and strengthen existing ones.

This may involve a combination of different approaches, such as mentoring, coaching and participation in training programmes.

Mentoring is an effective form of leadership development that involves collaborating with an experienced mentor who can provide guidance, advice and support. A mentor can share her experience and knowledge, help you identify opportunities for growth, and provide you with constructive feedback on your performance as a leader. By establishing a mentoring relationship, you can learn from another person's experience and accelerate your own development as a leader.

Coaching is another powerful tool for developing leadership skills. Unlike mentoring, which focuses on the exchange of experience and knowledge, coaching focuses on personal and professional growth through the exploration of goals, values and skills. A coach can help you identify your strengths and areas of development, establish clear objectives and design an action plan to achieve your goals. Additionally, a coach can provide support and accountability as you work to improve your leadership skills.

In addition to mentoring and coaching, participating in specific training programs can also be beneficial for developing leadership skills. These programs can address a variety of topics, such as leadership, communication, teamwork, change management, and problem solving. By participating in training programs, you can learn new techniques and strategies, share experiences with other leaders, and gain fresh perspectives on leadership and management.

Once you have developed an action plan for your leadership skills development, it is important to implement it in a consistent and committed manner. This may involve dedicating time and resources to engage in development activities, setting clear and measurable goals, and seeking opportunities to practice and apply new skills in your daily work.

Additionally, it is important to maintain an open and receptive mindset to continuous learning. Leadership is a lifelong journey, and there are always opportunities to grow and improve as a leader. Maintain an attitude of curiosity and a willingness to learn from your experiences, both positive and negative, and constantly look for ways to improve your performance and make an even greater contribution as a leader.

Developing leadership skills is an ongoing process that requires self-assessment, commitment, and a well-defined strategy. By identifying specific areas of improvement, developing an action plan, and leveraging resources such as mentoring, coaching, and training programs, you can strengthen your leadership skills and reach your full potential as a leader. By keeping an open mind to continuous learning and committing to your own growth and development, you can become a more effective and successful leader.

Balance between work and personal life.

In the modern world, where work demands are increasingly demanding and technology keeps us connected 24 hours a day, finding a balance between work and personal life has become essential for well-being and mental health. As a leader, it's especially important that you set an example in this regard, as your team will look to your behavior as a guide for theirs. Reflecting on how you can achieve a healthy balance between your work responsibilities and your personal well-being, and developing strategies to maintain that balance over time, is crucial to your success and that of your team.

First, it is important to recognize that work-life balance is an ongoing and dynamic process. There is no one formula that works for everyone, as each person has different needs, responsibilities and priorities. Therefore, it is important that you take the time to reflect on what is important to you in your personal and professional life, and how you can integrate those two areas harmoniously.

A key strategy for achieving a healthy work-life balance is to set clear, realistic boundaries. This may involve setting defined work hours and adhering to them as much as possible, as well as setting limits on availability outside of working hours. It is important to communicate these boundaries clearly and directly to your team and superiors, so they can respect your personal time and space.

Additionally, it is important to prioritize your activities and responsibilities both at work and in your personal life. This may involve identifying the most important and urgent tasks and projects at work, and setting aside specific time in your schedule to accomplish them efficiently. Likewise, in your personal life, it's important to identify the activities and commitments that are most meaningful and fulfilling for you, and make sure you dedicate time to them regularly.

Another important strategy for maintaining a healthy work-life balance is to practice self-care regularly. This can include activities such as exercising, meditating, spending time outdoors, connecting with friends and loved ones, and engaging in hobbies and pastimes that bring you joy and fulfillment. Prioritizing your physical, mental, and emotional well-being will help you stay healthy and energized to meet challenges at work and in your personal life.

Additionally, it is important to learn to delegate tasks and responsibilities both at work and at home. As a leader, it can be tempting to try to do everything yourself, but this can lead to unnecessary burnout and stress. Learning to trust your team and assign tasks based on each member's skills and abilities will allow you to free up time and energy to focus on the activities that are most important and meaningful to you.

Open and honest communication also plays a key role in maintaining a healthy work-life balance. It is important to talk to your team and your superiors about your needs and expectations in terms of working hours and availability outside of working hours. Likewise, it's important to communicate with loved ones about your work responsibilities and how they can support you in your efforts to achieve a healthy balance.

Finally, it is important to remember that work-life balance is not achieved overnight and requires continuous and constant effort. It's normal to have times when you feel overwhelmed or unbalanced, but it's important to be patient and compassionate with yourself. As you commit to finding a healthy work-life balance and develop strategies to maintain it over time, you'll find that you can achieve your professional goals while maintaining your personal well-being and happiness.

The World Waits for Your Leadership!

Chapter 8:
Personal Development and Self-knowledge.

Emotional self-awareness.

Emotional self-awareness is a cornerstone of effective leadership. It is about the ability to recognize and understand our own emotions, as well as their effects on our behavior and the people around us. In the management field, this skill is essential, since an emotionally intelligent leader can positively influence his team, make better decisions and maintain stronger and healthier work relationships.

Understanding our own emotions involves recognizing not only what we feel, but also why we feel it. This requires a high degree of self-exploration and reflection. An emotionally aware leader is able to identify and name his or her emotions accurately, whether in situations of tension, stress, joy, or any other emotional state. This ability not only allows us to know ourselves better, but also gives us the opportunity to regulate our emotions more effectively.

The influence of emotional self-awareness on leadership is profound. When a leader understands his own emotions, he can anticipate how these emotions may affect his behavior and her decisions. For example, if a leader knows that he tends to get frustrated when things don't go as planned, he can take proactive steps to prevent that frustration from negatively affecting his ability to lead. Instead of reacting impulsively, a self-aware leader can choose to respond in a more calm and thoughtful manner.

Additionally, emotional self-awareness allows leaders to recognize how their emotions can influence others. Leaders are role models for their teams, and their emotions can be contagious. A leader who displays calm and confidence in times of crisis can help reassure their team and foster a sense of security and stability. Likewise, a leader who demonstrates empathy and understanding can strengthen emotional bonds within the team and foster an environment of collaboration and mutual support.

Emotional self-awareness is also critical to developing effective work relationships. When leaders are able to recognize and express their own emotions authentically, this creates an environment of trust and transparency in the team. Team members feel more comfortable sharing their own emotions and concerns, which facilitates open and honest communication. Additionally, a leader who is aware of his own strengths and weaknesses can delegate tasks more effectively and collaborate more productively with his team.

To develop emotional self-awareness, leaders can adopt a variety of practices and techniques. This may include regularly practicing mindfulness and self-reflection, seeking honest feedback from colleagues and team members, and participating in personal development and emotional leadership programs. Additionally, leaders can work on improving their emotional intelligence, developing skills such as empathy, emotional self-regulation, and conflict management.

Emotional self-awareness is a critical skill for effective leadership. Understanding our own emotions allows us to make better decisions, positively influence others, and develop strong, healthy work relationships. By cultivating emotional self-awareness, leaders can improve their ability to lead successfully in any environment and meet leadership challenges with confidence and clarity.

Time management and prioritization.

Time management and prioritization are essential skills for any leader looking to optimize their productivity and achieve their goals efficiently. In a dynamic and fast-paced business environment, knowing how to properly manage time and assign the right priorities can make the difference between success and failure. In this analysis, we will explore various techniques and strategies that leaders can employ to improve their time management and their ability to prioritize tasks effectively.

One of the first steps in time management is to identify and understand how time is currently used. This may involve keeping detailed records of daily activities over a period of time to identify patterns and areas for improvement. By evaluating how time is distributed among different tasks and activities, leaders can identify areas of time waste and opportunities to optimize their use of time.

Once this initial assessment has been completed, leaders can begin to implement specific techniques to improve their time management. An effective strategy is to use planning and organization tools, such as electronic planners, to-do lists, and time management apps, to help stay organized and focused on priority tasks. These tools can help break down large projects into smaller, more manageable tasks, making them easier to track and complete.

In addition to using planning tools, leaders can also benefit from time management techniques like the Pomodoro technique, which involves working in short, focused blocks of time followed by short breaks. This technique can help maintain focus and productivity by providing regular intervals of rest and renewal of energy. Similarly, the Eisenhower technique, which involves ranking tasks based on their urgency and importance, can help you effectively prioritize activities and minimize procrastination.

In addition to using specific time management techniques, leaders can also benefit from adopting a proactive mindset toward planning and organizing. This may involve anticipating and planning future tasks and responsibilities in advance, rather than waiting until the last minute to address them. By setting clear goals and realistic deadlines for tasks, leaders can reduce the stress and anxiety associated with time management and increase their effectiveness and efficiency at work.

Another important aspect of time management and prioritization is learning to say "no" effectively. Leaders are often faced with multiple demands and requests competing for their time and attention, and it is crucial to be able to set clear boundaries and prioritize tasks based on their importance and contribution to overall goals. This may involve learning to delegate less important or urgent tasks to other team members, or simply rejecting commitments that don't align with current priorities.

Time management and prioritization are critical skills for any leader looking to maximize their productivity and achieve their goals effectively. By identifying how time is currently used, implementing specific time management techniques, adopting a proactive mindset toward planning and organizing, and learning to say "no" effectively, leaders can improve their ability to effectively manage time. and achieve success in their leadership roles.

Resilience and stress management.

In today's dynamic work environment, resilience and stress management are vital skills for leaders who want to maintain high performance and effectively lead their teams. The ability to face challenges, adapt to adverse situations and remain calm under pressure are essential aspects of resilience, while effective stress management helps maintain a healthy work-life balance. In this analysis, we will explore key strategies for building resilience and managing stress in demanding work environments.

A fundamental strategy for developing resilience is to cultivate a positive and optimistic mindset. Resilient leaders tend to view challenges as opportunities for learning and growth, rather than insurmountable obstacles. Adopting a positive attitude can help counteract the impact of stress and promote a greater ability to deal with challenges effectively. This may involve practicing gratitude, looking for the positive side of difficult situations, and cultivating hope and confidence in yourself and others.

In addition to maintaining a positive mindset, it is important to develop effective coping skills to manage stress and adversity. This may include relaxation techniques such as deep breathing and meditation, which can help reduce anxiety and promote calm and mental clarity. Likewise, regular exercise and a healthy diet can have a significant impact on reducing stress and improving overall well-being.

Another important strategy for building resilience is to cultivate a strong support network. Resilient leaders often rely on the support of colleagues, friends, family, and mentors who can offer guidance, emotional support, and helpful perspectives during difficult times. Seeking support from others and maintaining strong social connections can provide a source of strength and resilience in times of adversity.

In addition to developing individual coping skills, leaders can also benefit from adopting effective self-management practices to avoid burnout and maintain a healthy work-life balance. This may involve setting clear boundaries between work and personal time, delegating tasks when possible, and learning to unwind and relax outside of work. Prioritizing self-care and spending time on activities that encourage relaxation and well-being can help prevent burnout and promote long-term mental and emotional health.

Finally, it is important to remember that resilience and stress management are skills that can be developed and improved with time and practice. Although it is natural to experience stress and face challenges at work, learning how to handle these situations effectively can make a big difference in a leader's ability to remain strong and resilient in the face of adversity. By implementing key strategies such as maintaining a positive mindset, developing effective coping skills, and cultivating a strong support network, leaders can strengthen their resilience and manage stress more effectively in demanding work environments.

Creativity and lateral thinking.

Creativity and lateral thinking are essential skills for leaders who want to innovate, effectively solve problems, and make strategic decisions in an ever-changing business environment. The ability to think creatively and view situations from new perspectives can provide a significant competitive advantage and open new opportunities for growth and success. In this discussion, we will examine several ways leaders can foster creativity and lateral thinking in problem-solving and decision-making.

A key strategy to foster creativity and lateral thinking is to create an environment that encourages experimentation and innovation. This may involve encouraging team members to come up with new ideas and solutions, regardless of how risky or out of the ordinary they may seem. Leaders can foster an environment of trust and psychological safety where employees feel comfortable sharing their ideas without fear of being judged or criticized. This can open the door to new ways of thinking and generate innovative solutions to business challenges.

In addition to creating an environment that fosters creativity, leaders can also encourage collaboration and idea sharing among team members. This may involve hosting brainstorming sessions or team-building meetings where employees are encouraged to share their thoughts and perspectives on a particular problem or project. By collaborating and combining different points of view and skills, teams can generate more creative and effective solutions than if they worked individually.

Another strategy to encourage creativity and lateral thinking is to challenge conventional assumptions and norms. Leaders can encourage team members to question the status quo and consider new ways to address problems and opportunities. This may involve asking provocative questions, such as "Why do we do it this way?" or "What would happen if we explored this radical idea?" By challenging long-held assumptions and opening minds to new possibilities, leaders can inspire creativity and innovative thinking.

In addition to encouraging creativity in the problem-solving process, leaders can also apply specific lateral thinking techniques to generate innovative ideas. This can include methods such as design thinking, which involves approaching problems from the user's perspective and seeking solutions centered on people's needs and experiences. Similarly, the technique of lateral thinking, popularized by Edward de Bono, encourages looking for solutions outside the usual path and exploring different approaches to approaching a problem.

Finally, it is important to provide time and space for creativity to flourish. Leaders can allow team members free time to explore personal ideas and projects, as well as encourage a healthy work-life balance that allows employees to recharge and find inspiration outside of the work environment. By providing an environment conducive to creativity and lateral thinking, leaders can cultivate a culture of innovation and generate creative and effective solutions to business challenges.

Creativity and lateral thinking are critical skills for leaders seeking to innovate, solve complex problems, and make strategic decisions in an ever-evolving business environment. By creating an environment that encourages experimentation and collaboration, challenging conventional assumptions, and applying specific lateral thinking techniques, leaders can inspire creativity and innovative thinking in their teams and generate effective, transformative solutions.

Emotional intelligence development.

Developing emotional intelligence is crucial for leaders who want to relate better to others and lead more effectively in today's business environment. Emotional intelligence involves the ability to recognize, understand and manage one's own emotions, as well as to perceive and respond empathically to the emotions of others. In this analysis, we will explore how leaders can improve their emotional intelligence to strengthen their leadership and interpersonal skills.

One way to improve emotional intelligence is to increase emotional awareness, which involves recognizing and understanding one's own emotions. Leaders can practice regular self-assessment to identify and understand their own emotions, as well as the situations that trigger them. This may involve keeping an emotional journal, where leaders can record their emotions, thoughts and behaviors in different situations to identify patterns and areas for improvement. By increasing emotional awareness, leaders can develop a greater understanding of themselves and how their emotions influence their decisions and relationships with others.

Another important aspect of emotional intelligence is emotional self-regulation, which involves the ability to control and manage one's emotions effectively. Leaders can practice emotional regulation techniques, such as deep breathing, meditation, and positive visualization, to maintain calm and mental clarity in stressful or challenging situations. Additionally, leaders can learn to identify and address negative thoughts and emotional patterns that may interfere with their ability to make objective decisions and lead effectively.

In addition to developing emotional self-regulation, leaders can also improve their emotional intelligence by cultivating empathy toward others. Empathy involves the ability to put yourself in another person's shoes and understand their thoughts, feelings, and perspectives. Leaders can practice active listening and show genuine interest in the concerns and needs of others to strengthen their emotional connection with team members and foster an environment of trust and collaboration. By cultivating empathy, leaders can improve their interpersonal relationships and their ability to motivate and guide others effectively.

Another key component of emotional intelligence is the ability to manage social relationships effectively. This involves the ability to communicate clearly and effectively, resolve conflicts constructively, and work collaboratively as a team. Leaders can develop these skills by participating in leadership development programs that include training in communication skills, conflict resolution, and teamwork. Additionally, leaders can look for opportunities to practice these skills in real situations at work, such as leading team meetings, facilitating difficult discussions, or collaborating on joint projects.

Developing emotional intelligence is critical for leaders who want to relate better to others and lead more effectively in today's business environment. By increasing emotional awareness, practicing emotional self-regulation, cultivating empathy, and improving social skills, leaders can strengthen their emotional intelligence and improve their ability to influence, motivate, and guide others effectively. By doing so, they can create a more positive and productive work environment where employees feel valued, supported, and motivated to reach their full potential.

Chapter 9: Building and Managing Relationships.

Development of professional networks.

In today's business world, building and maintaining a strong professional network is essential for personal and professional growth. These networks not only offer professional development opportunities, but also provide support, guidance, and an invaluable source of knowledge and resources. In this analysis, we will explore the importance of professional networks and how they can contribute to the success of a leader in the business context.

First, professional networks provide a platform for the exchange of knowledge and experiences between colleagues and industry professionals. By connecting with people who have different backgrounds, skills, and perspectives, leaders can gain new ideas, up-to-date information on trends and best practices, and access to resources and opportunities that may not otherwise be available. This collaboration and knowledge sharing can be crucial to problem solving, innovation, and continued professional growth.

Additionally, professional networks offer opportunities to build strong, long-lasting relationships with colleagues, mentors, clients, and other industry leaders. These relationships can provide emotional support, advice and guidance in times of difficulty or uncertainty, as well as opportunities for collaboration and joint project development. By building authentic, trust-based relationships, leaders can strengthen their support network and expand their opportunities for long-term professional growth and success.

Additionally, professional networks can be an invaluable source of opportunities for professional development and career advancement. By connecting with influential professionals and thought leaders in the industry, leaders can access mentoring opportunities, training and development programs, and leadership positions that may otherwise be difficult to achieve. These connections can provide the boost needed to advance your career and achieve ambitious career goals.

In addition to offering professional development opportunities, professional networks can also be an important source of support and advice during periods of career transition or change. Whether they are seeking new career opportunities, facing challenges at work, or considering a career change, leaders can turn to their professional network for valuable guidance, advice, and references. This support network can be especially important during times of uncertainty or change in the work environment.

To build and maintain a strong professional network, leaders must dedicate time and effort to cultivating meaningful and authentic relationships with colleagues and industry professionals. This may involve participating in networking events, such as conferences, seminars, and trade shows, where they can meet new people and make meaningful connections. They can also use online platforms, such as LinkedIn, to connect with colleagues, follow thought leaders in the industry, and participate in professional groups and communities.

Additionally, it is important to stay in regular contact with network members, whether through in-person meetings, phone calls, or emails, to maintain relationships and strengthen professional ties. This may involve sharing news, updates, and professional achievements, as well as seeking opportunities for collaboration and mutual support. By staying active and engaged with their professional network, leaders can maximize the benefits and opportunities these connections can offer.

Building and maintaining a strong professional network is essential to the personal and professional growth of a leader in today's business world. These networks not only offer opportunities for professional development and career advancement, but they also provide support, guidance, and an invaluable source of knowledge and resources.

By dedicating time and effort to building meaningful, authentic relationships with colleagues and industry professionals, leaders can expand their opportunities for long-term career growth and success.

Negotiation and conflict resolution.

In the work environment, the ability to negotiate effectively and resolve conflicts constructively are essential skills for a leader. Negotiation is a process in which the parties involved seek to reach a mutually beneficial agreement, while conflict resolution involves addressing and resolving differences between individuals or groups in a way that promotes harmony and teamwork. In this analysis, we will explore techniques for effectively negotiating and constructively resolving conflict in the workplace.

A key technique for effective negotiation is proper preparation. Before entering into a negotiation, it is important to fully research and understand the issue at hand, as well as identify the negotiating objectives and points of all parties involved. This may involve gathering relevant information, analyzing options, and developing strategies to achieve the best possible results.

By being well prepared, a leader can increase his or her chances of negotiation success and make informed decisions that benefit all parties.

In addition to preparation, clear and effective communication is essential during the negotiation process. Leaders must be able to express their views and objectives clearly and directly, while actively listening to the concerns and perspectives of other parties involved. This requires empathetic listening skills, the ability to ask open-ended questions, and the skills to manage strong or conflicting emotions constructively. By encouraging open and transparent communication, leaders can facilitate a more fluid and collaborative negotiation process.

Another important technique for effective negotiation is the ability to find creative and win-win solutions. Instead of focusing solely on their own interests, leaders must seek solutions that meet the needs and concerns of all parties involved. This may involve exploring alternative options, mutual compromises and innovative solutions that allow all parties to achieve their objectives satisfactorily. By taking a collaborative, win-win approach, leaders can build strong, long-lasting relationships with colleagues and business partners.

In addition to negotiating effectively, leaders must also be skilled at conflict resolution. This involves addressing and resolving differences in a way that promotes mutual understanding, forgiveness and reconciliation between the parties involved. An important technique in conflict resolution is the ability to manage strong emotions and remain calm in difficult situations. This may involve stress management techniques, such as deep breathing, mindfulness, or using pauses to reflect before responding.

Additionally, it is important to address conflict proactively and constructively, rather than ignoring or avoiding it. Leaders must be willing to face problems head-on, seek to understand the concerns and perspectives of all parties involved, and work together to find solutions that meet the needs of all. This may require effective communication skills, empathy, and the ability to find common ground and mutual commitments.

Effective negotiation and conflict resolution are essential skills for a leader in the workplace. By adequately preparing, communicating clearly and effectively, seeking creative and win-win solutions, and addressing conflict proactively and constructively, leaders can foster strong, constructive relationships with colleagues, business partners, and customers. By mastering these skills, leaders can contribute to the success and effectiveness of their teams and organizations overall.

Empathy and interpersonal understanding.

Empathy and interpersonal understanding are fundamental skills in effective leadership and team management. These skills allow leaders to genuinely connect with their employees, understand their perspectives and emotions, and foster a collaborative and compassionate work environment. In this analysis, we will explore how to develop the capacity for empathy and interpersonal understanding to improve interpersonal relationships and team performance.

First, it's important to understand what empathy actually entails. Empathy goes beyond simply understanding the emotions of others; It involves the ability to put yourself in another person's shoes, see the world from their perspective, and respond in a compassionate and caring way. This requires active listening, paying attention to non-verbal cues, and showing genuine interest in the experiences and feelings of others.

To develop empathy, leaders can practice active listening and mindfulness in their daily interactions. This involves spending time and mindfulness in conversations, showing genuine interest in what others are saying and asking open-ended questions to deepen your understanding. Additionally, leaders can practice empathy by seeking to understand the concerns and perspectives of others, even when they disagree with them.

In addition to active listening, empathy also involves the ability to show compassion and support toward others in times of difficulty or suffering. This may involve expressing sympathy, offering words of encouragement, or simply being present and available to offer emotional support. By demonstrating empathy in times of need, leaders can strengthen relationships and create a sense of connection and trust within the team.

Interpersonal understanding goes hand in hand with empathy and refers to the ability to understand and manage interpersonal dynamics within the team. This involves recognizing individual differences, communication styles and work preferences of team members, and adapting to them effectively. Leaders can develop interpersonal understanding by actively observing and listening to team members, identifying their strengths and areas of development, and providing the support necessary to maximize their potential.

Additionally, interpersonal understanding involves the ability to resolve conflicts constructively and promote a harmonious and collaborative work environment. This may involve facilitating difficult conversations, mediating disputes between team members, and fostering a culture of respect and tolerance within the team.

By managing conflict effectively, leaders can strengthen interpersonal relationships and promote a positive and productive work environment.

To develop empathy and interpersonal understanding, leaders can benefit from practices such as coaching, social skills training, and 360-degree feedback. These practices can help leaders identify their strengths and areas of improvement in terms of empathy and interpersonal understanding, and provide them with the tools and strategies necessary to develop these skills effectively.

Empathy and interpersonal understanding are essential skills in effective leadership and team management. By developing the ability to put themselves in the shoes of others, understand their points of view and emotions, and manage interpersonal dynamics effectively, leaders can strengthen interpersonal relationships, foster a collaborative and compassionate work environment, and improve the overall team performance.

Coaching and mentoring.

Coaching and mentoring are essential practices in the professional development and growth of team members in any organization. These strategies allow leaders to help their employees reach their full potential, providing them with guidance, support and resources to improve their skills and achieve their professional goals. In this analysis, we will explore the role of coaching and mentoring in the business context and how they can contribute to individual and collective success.

First, it is important to understand the difference between coaching and mentoring. Coaching focuses on developing specific skills and achieving short-term goals. It involves a more structured, performance-focused relationship, where the coach works with the employee to identify areas of improvement, set clear goals, and provide ongoing feedback and support to achieve those goals. On the other hand, mentoring is a more informal and long-term relationship, where a mentor shares his or her experience, knowledge and advice with the mentee to help them grow professionally and advance their career.

Coaching and mentoring can benefit both leaders and employees. For leaders, these practices offer the opportunity to develop leadership skills, improve talent retention, and promote a culture of learning and growth within the team. For employees, coaching and mentoring provide personalized guidance and support to develop skills, overcome challenges and advance their professional career.

One of the main advantages of coaching and mentoring is its personalized and individual-centered approach.

Through one-on-one sessions, leaders can identify their employees' strengths and weaknesses, as well as their professional goals and aspirations. With this information, they can design a personalized development plan that suits each individual's specific needs and goals, providing the support and guidance necessary to achieve success.

Additionally, coaching and mentoring encourage responsibility and self-direction in professional development. By empowering employees to take responsibility for their own growth and learning, leaders can foster a sense of ownership and commitment to professional development. This can lead to a higher level of motivation and commitment on the part of employees, as well as an increase in job satisfaction and overall team performance.

Another advantage of coaching and mentoring is its ability to provide effective and constructive feedback. Through regular coaching sessions and mentoring meetings, leaders can offer specific, personalized feedback on employee performance and progress, as well as suggestions for improvement and professional growth. This timely and relevant feedback can help employees identify areas for improvement and take concrete steps to address them.

Additionally, coaching and mentoring can promote the development of soft skills and interpersonal competencies, which are increasingly important in today's work environment. Through coaching and mentoring sessions, employees can improve their communication, leadership, teamwork, and problem-solving skills, which can contribute to their long-term success in their professional roles.

Coaching and mentoring are essential practices in the professional development and growth of team members in any organization. These strategies offer an invaluable opportunity for leaders and employees alike, providing personalized guidance, support and resources to improve performance, achieve career goals and advance careers. By adopting a coaching and mentoring approach, leaders can cultivate an environment of continuous learning and growth, thereby promoting individual and collective success within the team and the organization as a whole.

Building high-performance teams.

Building high-performance teams is a fundamental task for any leader seeking sustainable success in their organization. These teams are not only able to consistently achieve goals and objectives, but they also cultivate a positive work environment, where members feel valued, motivated, and committed to collective success. In this analysis, we will explore key strategies for building and leading high-performing teams that work collaboratively and achieve exceptional results.

First, it is crucial to understand the importance of diversity in building high-performing teams. Diversity in terms of skills, experiences, backgrounds and perspectives enriches the team's talent pool and promotes creativity and innovation. By bringing together individuals with different strengths and complementary skills, an environment of continuous learning is fostered where members can share knowledge and experiences, and collaborate on effective problem-solving.

Additionally, it is essential to set clear goals and expectations from the beginning and align them with the organizational vision and objectives. High-performing teams have a clear understanding of what is expected of them and how their work contributes to the overall success of the organization. This gives them a sense of purpose and direction, motivating them to work toward common goals in a cohesive and committed manner.

Open and effective communication is another fundamental pillar in building high-performance teams. Leaders must foster an environment where transparent, honest and respectful communication is valued and practiced. This includes promoting a culture of constructive feedback, where team members feel safe sharing ideas, concerns and suggestions to improve teamwork and overall performance.

Additionally, leaders must foster an environment of trust and mutual respect within the team. Trust is the foundation of any effective relationship, and high-performing teams are no exception. Leaders must demonstrate integrity, honesty and consistency in their actions and decisions, and foster an environment where members feel safe sharing their ideas and opinions without fear of retaliation or judgment.

Collaboration and teamwork are essential elements in building high-performing teams. Leaders must foster an environment where collaboration among team members is valued and encouraged, recognizing and rewarding collective efforts and promoting a sense of camaraderie and mutual support. This may involve assigning projects and tasks that encourage collaboration and sharing of ideas, as well as celebrating team achievements collectively.

Additionally, leaders must invest in the professional development and personal growth of team members. This may involve providing training and development opportunities, establishing mentoring and coaching programs, and recognizing and rewarding exceptional performance. By investing in the growth and development of team members, leaders not only strengthen the team's skills and capabilities, but also promote a sense of commitment and loyalty to the organization.

Building high-performing teams is an ongoing process that requires constant commitment from leaders and team members. By adopting strategies that encourage diversity, establish clear goals, promote effective communication, foster trust and mutual respect, foster collaboration and teamwork, and promote personal and professional growth and development, leaders can create highly motivated teams. effective and capable of consistently achieving exceptional results.

Chapter 10: Innovation and Organizational Change.

Innovation culture.

Fostering a culture of innovation within an organization is crucial to staying relevant in an ever-changing business environment and driving long-term growth and competitiveness. A culture of innovation not only implies the generation of new ideas, but also the ability to implement them effectively and agilely. In this analysis, we will explore how leaders can foster an organizational culture that values innovation and fosters creativity among their teams.

First, it is essential that leaders establish a clear and shared vision of the importance of innovation within the organization. This involves effectively communicating the benefits of innovation and how it can lead to the company's long-term success. By articulating a compelling vision for innovation, leaders can inspire and motivate employees to contribute new ideas and creative solutions.

Additionally, leaders must create an environment that encourages experimentation and continuous learning. This may involve allowing failure as part of the innovation process, as long as valuable lessons are drawn from each experience. By promoting a culture of learning and growth, leaders can encourage employees to try new ideas and approaches without fear of failure, which can lead to the generation of innovative and disruptive solutions.

Collaboration and teamwork are also key elements in building a culture of innovation. Leaders should foster interdepartmental collaboration and create opportunities for employees from different areas and hierarchical levels to work together on innovation projects. This can help generate new perspectives and approaches, as well as foster a sense of ownership and commitment to the organization's innovation objectives.

Additionally, it is important to provide employees with the time, resources and space necessary to engage in creative and innovative activities. This may involve allocating specific time during the week for innovation projects, as well as providing access to tools and technologies that facilitate experimentation and collaboration. By investing in resources for innovation, leaders demonstrate their commitment to creating a culture that values and supports creativity and innovation.

Leaders can also foster innovation by recognizing and rewarding employees' creative thinking and innovative contributions. This may involve celebrating innovation-related successes and achievements, as well as providing incentives and development opportunities for those who contribute significantly to the generation of new ideas and solutions.

By recognizing and rewarding innovation, leaders reinforce desired behaviors and foster a culture in which creativity and innovation are valued and encouraged.

Additionally, leaders must act as role models and promote a leadership mindset that is open and receptive to new ideas and approaches. This may involve sharing personal experiences of innovation and showing vulnerability by acknowledging the challenges and obstacles they face in the innovation process. By demonstrating a personal commitment to innovation, leaders can inspire others to follow their example and actively contribute to the culture of innovation within the organization.

Fostering a culture of innovation is critical to the long-term success of any organization. Leaders play a crucial role in building this culture by establishing a clear and shared vision of the importance of innovation, creating an environment that encourages experimentation and learning, promoting collaboration and teamwork, and providing resources and support. for innovation, recognize and reward creativity and innovation, and act as role models for a leadership mindset that is open and receptive to new ideas and approaches. By adopting these strategies, leaders can cultivate an organizational culture that values innovation and encourages creativity, which can lead to the generation of innovative solutions and the long-term success of the organization.

Change management.

Managing change in an organization is a critical skill for leaders, as the business environment is constantly evolving and companies must adapt to stay competitive. However, implementing change within an organization can be a complex and challenging process, as it requires effective leadership and the ability to manage resistance to change. In this analysis, we will explore techniques to successfully lead organizational change processes and manage resistance to change effectively.

First, it is critical that leaders establish a clear and compelling vision for change and communicate this vision effectively to all members of the organization. Open and transparent communication about the reasons for the change, the objectives to be achieved and the impact it will have on the organization and employees is essential to generate support and commitment to the change process.

Additionally, leaders must involve employees in the change process, giving them the opportunity to participate in decision-making and contribute ideas and suggestions. By involving employees in the change process, leaders can help create a sense of ownership and commitment to the change, which can increase the likelihood of success of the change process.

It is important to recognize that change can generate resistance among employees, whether due to fear of the unknown, loss of familiarity, or a perceived threat to job security. Leaders must be aware of this resistance and develop strategies to manage it effectively. This may involve identifying the underlying causes of resistance to change, communicating openly and honestly about the benefits of the change, and providing support and resources to help employees adapt to the change.

Additionally, leaders must show empathy and understanding toward employees who experience resistance to change, acknowledging their concerns and providing the necessary support to help them overcome them. This may involve offering training and development opportunities to gain the skills needed to adapt to change, as well as providing guidance and mentoring to help employees manage the stress and uncertainty associated with change.

Change management also requires careful planning and effective execution. Leaders should develop a detailed plan to implement the change, including assigning roles and responsibilities, defining key deadlines and milestones, and identifying success metrics to evaluate the progress of the change.

Additionally, leaders must be prepared to adapt the change plan as necessary in response to challenges and obstacles that arise during the change process.

It is important to note that change management is an ongoing process and leaders must be prepared to face new challenges and adjust their strategies as the change process progresses. By remaining flexible and responsive to employee feedback and comments, leaders can continually improve their change management approaches and increase the chances of success of the organizational change process.

Change management is a critical skill for leaders as organizations seek to adapt and thrive in an ever-evolving business environment. By establishing a clear vision for change, involving employees in the process, managing resistance to change effectively, and executing change in a careful and planned manner, leaders can successfully lead organizational change processes and position their organizations to long-term success.

Strategic thinking.

Strategic thinking is an essential skill for leaders at any level of an organization. It involves the ability to comprehensively analyze the environment, identify emerging trends, evaluate resources and competencies, and make informed decisions that lead to the achievement of the organization's long-term objectives. In this analysis, we will explore the importance of strategic thinking in the context of leadership, as well as some key strategies for developing this skill.

In an increasingly complex and competitive business world, strategic thinking has become fundamental to organizational success. Leaders must be able to look beyond the immediate demands of the day and take a broader, long-term perspective. This involves understanding the vision and mission of the organization, as well as the challenges and opportunities it faces in its external and internal environment.

One of the main reasons why strategic thinking is so important is its role in formulating long-term goals. Strategic leaders not only focus on solving immediate problems, but also take into account how current decisions will affect the future of the organization. This involves identifying and prioritizing key areas of focus, setting clear and achievable goals, and developing detailed action plans to achieve those long-term goals.

Additionally, strategic thinking is essential for making informed and effective decisions. Strategic leaders are able to carefully evaluate available options, anticipate potential consequences, and make decisions that are aligned with the organization's goals and core values. This requires a deep understanding of the business environment, as well as an ability to analyze data and information critically and objectively.

To develop strategic thinking, leaders can adopt various strategies and techniques. One of them is to cultivate a mindset of continuous learning, actively seeking new ideas and perspectives and being open to changing your mind when necessary. Additionally, it is important to foster an environment that promotes open debate and the exchange of ideas, where diverse opinions are valued and respected.

Another key strategy is to develop the ability to think systemically and holistically. This involves considering not only the individual parts of a problem or situation, but also how they are interconnected and how they affect the system as a whole. By taking this broader perspective, leaders can more effectively identify the interdependencies and long-term implications of their decisions.

Additionally, it is important to develop strong analytical skills, including the ability to collect, organize, and analyze data effectively. This may involve using advanced analytical tools and techniques, as well as collaborating with experts in specific areas to obtain information and advice.

Last but not least, it is essential to develop effective communication skills to clearly and persuasively convey strategic ideas to all stakeholders. This involves being able to tailor the message to the audience and use multiple communication channels to ensure it is understood and accepted.

Strategic thinking is a critical skill for leaders in any organization. It involves the ability to formulate long-term objectives, make informed and effective decisions, and anticipate and respond proactively to changes in the business environment. By adopting key strategies to develop this skill, leaders can position themselves to meet future challenges and guide their organizations toward long-term success.

Adaptability and flexibility.

Adaptability and flexibility are critical skills in today's business world, where change is constant and rapid. Leaders who possess these qualities are able to meet challenges effectively, adjust to new circumstances, and take advantage of emerging opportunities. In this analysis, we will explore the importance of adaptability and flexibility in leadership, as well as some strategies for developing these skills.

In a dynamic and highly competitive business environment, the ability to adapt to change is essential for long-term success. Leaders who are adaptable and flexible are able to meet unexpected challenges and adjust their approach as necessary to achieve organizational goals. This means being able to change direction quickly when circumstances require it, without losing sight of the vision and core values of the organization.

One of the reasons why adaptability and flexibility are so important is their role in organizational resilience. Organizations that foster a culture of adaptability are better able to respond effectively to changes in the business environment and overcome the challenges they face. Leaders who are able to quickly adapt to new situations and learn from experience are critical to building this resilience.

Furthermore, adaptability and flexibility are essential for innovation and business growth. Leaders who are able to think creatively and explore new ideas are more likely to identify emerging opportunities and find innovative solutions to problems. The ability to adapt to new technologies, business models and market trends is essential to maintaining relevance and competitiveness in a constantly evolving business environment.

To develop adaptability and flexibility, leaders can adopt various strategies and techniques. One of them is to cultivate a mindset of continuous learning, being open to new ideas and perspectives and actively seeking opportunities to grow and develop personally and professionally. This may involve seeking feedback from colleagues and mentors, participating in professional development programs, and seeking opportunities to gain new skills and knowledge.

In addition, it is important to develop the ability to remain calm and composed in situations of pressure and stress. Leaders who are able to maintain composure and focus under pressure are more likely to make effective decisions and lead their teams to success. This may involve practicing stress management techniques, such as deep breathing, meditation, and regular exercise.

Another key strategy is to encourage collaboration and teamwork within the organization. Leaders who are able to build diverse and cohesive teams are more likely to find creative and effective solutions to the challenges they face. This involves fostering an environment where diverse opinions are valued and respected, the open exchange of ideas is encouraged, and collaboration and cooperation among team members is promoted.

Additionally, it is important to develop the ability to adapt to different work styles and personal preferences. Leaders who are able to adjust to the needs and communication styles of others are more likely to build strong and effective relationships with their colleagues and collaborators. This may involve being receptive to the opinions and perspectives of others, being flexible in assigning tasks and responsibilities, and being willing to compromise when necessary.

Adaptability and flexibility are fundamental skills in business leadership. Leaders who possess these qualities are able to face challenges with confidence, adjust to new circumstances, and take advantage of emerging opportunities. By adopting key strategies to develop these skills, leaders can position themselves to lead successfully in an ever-changing business environment.

Promotion of experimentation and learning.

Encouraging experimentation and continuous learning in an organization is essential to staying relevant in a constantly evolving business environment. In a world where change is the only constant, companies that can adapt quickly and learn from their experiences have a significant competitive advantage. In this analysis, we will explore the importance of promoting experimentation and continuous learning, as well as some key strategies for doing so effectively.

First, it is important to recognize that experimentation and learning are key drivers of innovation. By encouraging employees to try new ideas and approaches, an organization can discover new ways of doing things, identify opportunities to improve efficiency and effectiveness, and develop creative solutions to business challenges. Experimentation can also help an organization stay agile and responsive to changes in the market and business environment.

Additionally, encouraging experimentation and continuous learning can improve employee engagement and motivation. When employees have the opportunity to contribute ideas and participate in interesting and challenging projects, they are more engaged in their work and feel valued by the organization. Experimentation can also help develop a culture of trust and collaboration, where employees feel comfortable sharing ideas and working together to achieve common goals.

An effective way to encourage experimentation and continuous learning is to establish an environment that promotes curiosity and exploration. This may involve providing time and resources for employees to dedicate to research and development projects, as well as creating physical and virtual spaces where they can collaborate and share ideas.

It is also important to reward and recognize employee effort and creativity, even if the results are not always successful.

Additionally, it is important to foster a learning mindset throughout the organization, where failure is seen as an opportunity to learn and improve. Instead of punishing failure, leaders should encourage employees to reflect on their experiences, identify lessons learned, and apply those insights to improve in the future. This may involve celebrating successes and failures alike, and recognizing that learning often comes with adversity.

Another key strategy is to provide formal and informal professional development and training opportunities. This may include mentoring and mentoring programs, online and offline training courses, and opportunities to attend industry conferences and events. By investing in the professional development of employees, an organization can improve its ability to innovate and adapt to changes in the business environment.

Last but not least, it is important to foster a culture of feedback and constructive feedback, where employees feel comfortable giving and receiving honest and useful feedback. This can help identify areas for improvement and learning opportunities, as well as foster an environment of trust and openness where personal and professional growth and development are valued.

Encouraging experimentation and continuous learning is essential to driving innovation and growth in an organization. By encouraging employees to try new ideas, learn from their experiences, and work together to achieve common goals, an organization can remain agile and successfully adapt to changes in the business environment. By following some of the strategies mentioned above, leaders can create an environment conducive to experimentation and continuous learning, and set their organization up for long-term success.

Conclusion.

On the fascinating journey of business leadership, we have explored a vast landscape of concepts, strategies and skills aimed at driving success and excellence. From the very definition of leadership to building high-performing teams and managing organizational change, we have unraveled the complexities of leading and motivating others toward a common goal.

As we reflect on this journey, it is important to remember that leadership is not just a set of technical skills, but also an expression of our shared humanity. Behind every strategy and technique, there are real people with dreams, aspirations and challenges of their own. As leaders, our ability to connect with those people, understand their perspectives, and guide them to success is what really makes the difference.

In a world where the speed of change is dizzying and uncertainty is a constant, effective leadership becomes more crucial than ever. The challenges we face may be daunting, but they also offer opportunities to grow, innovate and prosper. As leaders, it is our duty to embrace those challenges with courage and determination, and lead with vision, integrity and compassion.

Ultimately, leadership is not just about achieving organizational goals and objectives, but also about inspiring and empowering others to reach their full potential. It's about building communities, fostering growth, and leaving a positive legacy that lasts far beyond our time in office.

So I invite you, to embrace your role as a leader with passion and commitment. Take advantage of the lessons learned in this book as a springboard toward more effective and meaningful leadership. Inspire others by your example, encourage innovation and continuous learning, and together, let's build a brighter, more promising future for all. The world awaits your leadership!

www.ingramcontent.com/pod-product-compliance
Lightning Source LLC
Chambersburg PA
CBHW071054240526
45471CB00015B/1938